BUYING
ANTIQUE FURNITURE

An Advisory

by

Lew Larason

SCORPIO PUBLICATIONS

1992

Printed in the United States of America

first Edition
Art work by the author
Front cover photography by the author
Rear cover photograph by Patti Guthrie

Library of Congress Cataloging-in-Publication Data

Larason, Lewis: 1932–
BUYING ANTIQUE FURNITURE: AN ADVISORY
Includes Bibliography
Library of Congress Catalog Card Number 91-90268
ISBN: 0-936099-02-X

Published by
SCORPIO PUBLICATIONS
2 East Butler Avenue
Chalfont, Pennsylvania
18914-3014

*To my Granddaughters, Tara and Sabrina White,
who ask such wonderful questions.*

Contents

ACKNOWLEDGMENTS

Anyone who reads will notice that writers tend to vary considerably as to whom they acknowledge and thank.

Without help, it would be nearly impossible to put together a book such as this. However, when all is said and done, it is up to the author to take responsibility.

Since this isn't a one-person effort, I want to mention my appreciation to the many publications which have used my articles through the years, especially Wolfe Publications, publisher of THE NEW YORK-PENNSYLVANIA COLLECTOR, in Fishers, New York, and their many subscribers who read me.

I always will be grateful to my high school shop teacher, John Fisher, who felt I had woodworking talent, to Dr. Corydon Crooks, who became my mentor when I began my apprenticeship with the late George Nakashima, and to so many others who have given me advice and encouragement through the years.

A special thanks to my wife, Patti. She has been relentless, all the time knowing that she would have to edit my scribbles and notes, "translating" them into English! In addition, to J. A. Kirk, my proofreader, thank you. And, there are two special people who don't know one another—a big thank you to Charlie and to Kay; without folks such as you, this undertaking wouldn't have been possible.

I dare not leave out the family cats, who so graciously allow me to live in their home, therefore enabling me to have a place to work and write; after all, that does buy cat food!

And, let me not forget God; if we weren't blessed with the talent to write and read, it would be a pretty sad world.

PREFACE

After nearly four decades of working with American antique furniture, I felt I might be able to help some buyers of this popular furniture. So many people don't know what they are looking for, looking at, what questions to ask, or to whom to address any questions they do have.

If this lead-in sounds confusing, believe me, it is nothing compared to a novice trying to buy a piece of antique furniture. There are so many pit-falls, so many misleading statements, and so many implications, with so few factual statements; that the buyer isn't sure who or what to believe. Often, these buyers are "left on their own" to make the final decision, one they may have to live with for many years. Since there is so little guidance when it comes to buying antique furniture, there are a lot of mistakes made.

Some people selling antique furniture aren't sure what they have; so, they are very quiet or careful about what they say regarding a given item when there is someone interested in buying it, someone who asks questions.

It is my hope that this book will help both the buyer and seller to develop more knowledge about something in which both are interested. If nothing else, perhaps this volume will pique your desire for knowledge, for learning more about the subject in which you apparently have some interest, or you wouldn't be reading this page!

As you read the following, please keep in mind that no book is the "last word". There is information, and therefore, knowledge to be gained everywhere; no one person is *the* expert. However, taken together, they offer the reader a combination of views and knowledge that is worth having.

Read and learn!

WHAT ARE YOUR RIGHTS
AS AN ANTIQUES BUYER?

In order to give the reader some insight on the subject, I informally interviewed two Pennsylvania attorneys before writing this, Tim Tammany, a friend who practices in Philadelphia, and John Larason, my nephew. Both pointed out that their comments were influenced by Pennsylvania laws, and that if someone feels he needs professional legal assistance, he should contact a local lawyer. Also, this is more a personal opinion than legal advice; so, before you quote me in court, please check with a local attorney!

What are my rights when I buy an antique? This is a good question, and one that I'm sure many collectors wonder about, whether they buy from dealers, privately, or at auction. I have been buying, selling, and restoring antique furniture since the mid-1950s, and can tell you that in my early years as a buyer, people were always passing off things to me which I would find out later were not what I had thought they were. In most cases, I took my licks, and learned from the errors.

As time went on and I learned more, I didn't make as many mistakes. Then, suddenly, I was aware that once again, people were trying to pass bad items on to me; but now, it was to test me because I had become one of the "old timers" in this business; again, I have to be very careful. So, as you can see, you never are immune from such activity. The possibility of buying a fake, reproduction, or reworked item is always there, even from reliable people who may not know what they have.

How do you protect yourself? First and foremost, know what you are examining. You gain knowledge by reading, asking questions, paying attention, and, sometimes, by making mistakes. When in doubt, have an expert whom you trust check out the item for you. It is better to pay a little money before you make an error than to spend a lot of money on a mistake. Think about this!

Now, what are your rights as a buyer? They may vary, depending on you. Let's say you are buying from an antiques dealer. Get a sales slip, or bill of sale. Ask about the return policy. And, remember this:

the more information which appears on that piece of paper, the more rights you have as a buyer.

For example, if you buy a Windsor chair, and the only information on the slip is "one chair, $125, paid," what rights do you have when someone who collects Windsors looks at it and says, "That's a reproduction, and a bad one at that, worth about $50 in a used furniture store?" Although you thought it was an early chair, you didn't ask the dealer to put the approximate age on the slip because you didn't want to seem a novice. So, there you are with a slip which only states that you purchased a chair and that you paid $125 for it. When you try to take the chair back, the dealer may point out that there is nothing wrong with it, and that no mention of age appears on the sales slip. That dealer has a good point!

Many would either give you your money back or give you credit; but, not every dealer. After all, you are an adult, and should have seen what you were buying. If you bought the chair from a known antiques dealer who advertises antiques for sale, and has an antique shop or displays at antiques shows, you may be expected to "assume" the dealer sells only antiques. But, you are on shaky ground.

If the dealer won't take back the chair, and you feel you're right, this may be a case for small claims court. In some states, I believe you don't need an attorney; but, check in your area first. And, be prepared for a fight. How much is your principle worth?

If this scenario had started out differently, it most likely would end differently. For example, if the dealer had written on your sales slip something such as "one Windsor chair, C. 1800, original condition, $125-paid," and you were able to prove it to be a thirty-year-old reproduction, you definitely have a good case for returning the chair, most likely with no problem except some hard feelings. You might have been a little suspicious because the chair was priced so low, but with the information on the sales slip, you should be more protected.

What all of this says to the buyer is that the more information you can get on your sales slip, the more protection you have. Little or no information tilts a decision in favor of the seller.

Be aware that antiques dealers aren't the only ones from whom you must protect yourself. When you purchase antiques privately, you need to be especially careful. Many times, I've looked at items in private homes which I recognized as fakes, reproductions, or heavily reworked pieces. And, the seller has told me that someone appraised them, and the prices are right! I know they aren't; but, rather than start an argument, I just leave.

If you do decide to buy privately, and you are told the item has been appraised, get a copy of the appraisal or at least ask who did it. Again, get as much information written on a sales slip as possible before you pay for anything. That is your only protection. Different laws apply to antiques dealers as merchants and to private sellers. After all, private sellers don't have their business reputations to protect when you try to return something after you've found out it wasn't what you were told. Again, check with a local attorney.

Conversely, if you "steal" something from someone, even paying their asking price, then turn around and sell the item for an incredible profit, you may have to share your large profit with the seller, at least in some states under certain laws and in some circumstances. So, be fair and honest; and, expect the same from the seller by getting all pertinent information on your sales slip.

Most dealers and other sellers of antiques are honest and want you to be happy with your purchase in the hope that you will be back in the future for something else; so, if the seller doesn't offer the information you need to protect yourself, it's up to you to ask for it. Have everything you want to know written out for you, preferably on your sales slip, since both you and the seller should have a copy of this document. Then, you may be protected even further since the omission of information could be interpreted as misrepresentation.

If you're looking at a country work table with deep skirts and a small overhang, and want to buy it only if your chairs will be usable with it, have the seller write on the slip that if you can't use the table with your chairs, you may return it for a full refund. Some sellers may not like to do that; and, indeed, some may not. That's when you must decide whether to leave the table where it is or take a chance, knowing you will not be able to return it under these circumstances.

There is the phrase *implied warranty.* If you buy a chest of drawers, it is expected that you will be able to use the item for the purpose for which it was intended. The same can be applied to a chair. When purchasing a chair, unless otherwise stated, you should expect to use the chair for its intended purpose. If you can't use an item for its intended purpose, and hadn't discussed that with the seller, you may have difficulty returning it. Implied warranty only applies when both parties understand what is being said.

In spite of popular belief, all antiques dealers are not crooks; and, they do not steal all of their merchandise and then try to sell it at exhorbitant prices. Most are honest business-people, generally with a great deal of knowledge. However, as with any profession, there are a few we'd rather were in another business!

There are also some dealers who just do not know as much as they think they do; unfortunately, they don't know that. These few are the ones you have to protect yourself from. We all do! And, among the private sellers, there are very few who really know enough to be selling antiques, unless they have a professional helping them.

So, along with knowledge, and knowing when you don't know, your best protection when buying is to get as much written out as possible, including the name, address, and phone number of the seller. Be wary of "cash only" and "no receipts"; if an error is made, you have no recourse. Your rights are very simple—the more information you have written out during a sales transaction, the more protection you have.

And, remember, sellers have rights too! If a piece is everything it is supposed to be, but you have just "changed your mind," that's hardly the seller's fault; and, you really have no right to return the item. You could ask; and, the seller might be obliging, but certainly is not required to take back the piece. You both have rights; and both of you should recognize that and protect yourselves accordingly. "CAVEAT EMPTOR!"

ADVISORY

INTRODUCTION

Do you know what a period piece of furniture is? How about a Centennial piece? Do you know the difference between a fake and a reproduction? Do you care? You should if you, in any way, are involved with antique furniture. It doesn't matter whether you are an antiques dealer, a collector, or a casual observer, if you don't know the language, you can't play the game!

Collecting goes back nearly as far as history. In the United States, collecting antiques started coming to life during the Philadelphia Centennial exhibition in 1876. That exhibition stirred up interest in our past; it was the beginning. By the mid 20th century, antique collecting had a good footing. Today it is the "in" thing to collect antiques. This being the case, let's go over some of the words you might hear while visiting an antiques shop, an antiques show, or your next cocktail party.

ANTIQUE: If you were to ask a group of "antiquers" what this word means, you'd most likely get as many answers as there are people gathered. The word is a noun, and came into usage about 1530; it means a number of things, including, "An item of ancient times, or an item from an earlier period than the present". According to various customs laws, a piece must be at least 100 years old to justify the title antique. However, in 1930, a United States tariff act exempted from duty, "Artistic antiquities, collections in illustration of the progress of the arts, objects of art of educational value or ornamental character, which shall have been produced prior to the year 1830". This date was appropriate, since that is about the end of traditionally handmade items and the beginning of industrialization. If this 1830 date was used today, many antiques shops and shows would be pretty sparse. It would be difficult to hold the line on that date for most of us, especially with non-furniture items. Because of the interest in collecting antique furniture, finding pre-1830 pieces that the average buyer can afford is becoming quite a challenge. So you need to know as much as possible when searching for early pieces.

Collecting antique furniture has become a big business which includes buying, selling, restoring, trading, writing, photographing, insuring, appraising, storing, reproducing, and on and on. Then, there is the black market of fakes! Big business indeed!

It is surprising, almost refreshing, to go nearly any place today and find a person who isn't interested in antiques! I overhear people in stores and restaurants talking about antiques, about something they just purchased, something their grandmother left them, or about a friend who just made a good buy. Most publications I see on the newsstand have something to say about collecting, antiques, old, or "the country look". The amount of misinformation I see and hear is very upsetting. A lot of the items referred to as antique date from the 1920s and 1930s. Sorry folks; I can't refer to these as antiques!

Frankly, I like the 1830 cut-off date. However, being realistic, I would push the date to the mid-1860s for simple country pieces. However, if we were to do that, we'd eliminate the early Victorian furniture, which would create a large void in the antiques business. So, what is an antique? It depends upon whom you ask. Different groups of people in different parts of the country have different definitions for the same word. In new England, a piece of furniture made during the Civil War would be just old; however, that same piece in Utah would be considered "an old antique".

What is a genuine antique? Fakes aside, authenticating a piece isn't always easy. There is only the expert's knowledge to make the final judgment; and, experts don't always agree! In rare instances, a piece of furniture may be signed and dated by its maker; that's great, as long as it isn't bogus! Again, an educated guess is all that most of us have to go on. In this field, trusted experts are your best allies, followed closely by your own knowledge. There is so much to learn; and there are so many pitfalls. The average buyer of antique furniture can get into a great deal of trouble really fast if not very careful! Just remember, you can't know too much when buying antique furniture!

I guess, for most of us, an antique is what we want it to be, depending upon where we live, what our friends call antique, and just how old we want our antiques to be! The following is some history on antique furniture, which may or may not relate to what you call an antique, or what you live with; but, this information should come in handy at some point in time.

WHAT IS A PERIOD PIECE? When someone says to you, "It's a period piece", do you know what you're being told? If the person knows what he's talking about, he means the piece of furniture was made during the time of its design or style. You'll need to know when the periods were, what was made during that time, and what materials were used. If you listen to everyone, you're going to get very confused! You'll hear names such as Jacobean, William and Mary, Queen Anne, Georgian, Chippendale, Adam, Hepplewhite, Sheraton, Regency, and Victorian. What do these names have in common? They're all English. And although they indicate English design and manufacture, there were items being made in the Colonies at the same time of similar designs. This is where knowledge comes in—to be able to tell if an item is of the period, and if it was made in England or in America.

Because of the diversity of immigrants coming here, the furniture of early America was of many lands, with each Colony having its own furniture and way of making furniture. In other words, each group of settlers brought to their isolated settlements their own crafts from their homelands. And since they didn't get to travel around, their idea of furniture design didn't change much from what they brought with them. People of many countries came to the shores of the New World. They included Swedes, French, Germans, Spanish, and Dutch; but, the most predominant were English. There were two main types of English settlers coming to Colonial America, the "royal-grant" wealthy who settled in the South, and the Puritans, who settled in New England. The Dutch in the Hudson Valley area of New York were greatly influenced by British merchants; but the Swedes and Germans of the Delaware Valley area weren't. This explains why the early Pennsylvania items are so different from those of the rest of the Colonies.

17th CENTURY: EARLY COLONIAL PERIOD. The Puritans who settled in New England brought a few of their Jacobean items with them. Although they kept the basic design, when they started to make furnishings, they used native woods, which included pine, oak, birch, and maple. These woods were a little different from the materials used in the "Mother Country", which is the best way to tell the pieces apart. In the South, the wealthier settlers imported much of the furniture they used during the earliest periods. In the Delaware Valley, the Swedes and Germans made most of their furniture using the styles they remembered from their homeland. They used local woods such as poplar and walnut. Because of Germanic, peasant influence, much of their furniture was painted and highly decorated. This also is true with some of the earliest Dutch pieces from the Hudson Valley area. However, British influence soon changed Hudson Valley furniture.

18th CENTURY. In the 18th century the Colonies were producing more and better cabinetmakers; also, there was more wealth with which to hire them. Through the century, there were many styles; the most prominent was Queen Anne. This style has become a generalization, using cabriole legs, shell carving, pad feet and the cyma curve. By mid-century, the fine cabinetmakers from Boston, New York, Philadelphia, and Newport were producing furniture as good as, if not better than, most of that of the English cabinetmakers.

From the mid to late 18th century, Chippendale style dominated the design scene. However, after the war, the Colonial period was over; and the old English designs no longer were in favor. What followed is referred to as the Federal Period; although also English, Adam, Hepplewhite, and Sheraton dominated the furniture design field. Their pieces were finer and more delicate than the heavy, often ornately carved pieces to which many were accustomed.

19th CENTURY. In the early 19th century, there was the Empire Period. The earliest designs weren't too bad; but, by the 1830s or so, a heavier, more massive style took over. The furniture designers of the early 19th century had to change as tastes changed; and, to quote someone else, "There is no accounting for taste". Through this period, we see Sheraton, Phyfe, and Hitchcock trying to keep some class in their designs, as Victorian designs and tastes took over, and industrialization of the civilized world expanded. Fads, revivals, and other changes moved so quickly that it was nearly impossible to keep up with all of them; there were so many!

Some of the better designs and manufactured pieces of these later periods have survived. They are what some people collect today as Victorian.

During all of these periods, there were reproduction, fake, Centennial and revival pieces. And, there are items which were made to replace lost or damaged ones, such as a set of chairs which started out as six. Several years later two, four, or more were made to match so the set could be expanded. If a good chairmaker made the new chairs, the later ones would be hard to identify from the originals. There is a lot to know; and a lot to learn.

Now that you have your own idea of what the word "antique" means, let's look at the different periods of antique furniture. I guess, if we wanted to, we could go back to the "furniture" used in the earliest caves: a stump of wood or a smooth rock; but, I want to concentrate on furniture used in the New World, America, from the mid 17th century, items the new settlers brought here and made here, up to the early 20th century. The fact that these early travelers were met by natives, who had a type of furniture of their own, will not be discussed here.

17th CENTURY: PILGRIM PERIOD or EARLY COLONIAL. Generally this early period is referred to as Jacobean, which is defined as "Of, relating to, or characteristic of James I of England or his age." The word came into common usage about 1844. James I reigned from 1603–25. As with most "periods", the furniture style which is called by a certain name runs long beyond the time for which it was named. Since most of the earliest settlers coming to these shores were English, with few exceptions, the early furniture styles were named after either the reigning monarch in England or after an English designer who influenced the furniture buyers and makers of a certain period in time. So, as you can see, most of the early furniture was English, or English influenced. There are some exceptions which I will cover later.

Most of us aren't likely to run into a piece of Jacobean furniture at a local auction or antiques shop. And, if we did, we'd be so suspicious, we most likely would leave it right where we saw it. However, you never know. About 1965, I was offered a large, very dark oak, heavily carved chest; I thought it was ugly; and, I just had seen some new, imported "antique chests" of dark oak at a local shop; so, I passed up this piece. After I did a bit of research and discussed the chest with an older dealer friend, we decided it should be looked at again. Too late! The item had been sold; to this day, I still don't know whether I passed up a good reproduction or one of "the" buys of my career as an antiques dealer. Looking back, I suspect it was an honest Hadley chest, dating from about 1690. My main reason for not buying it was lack of knowledge, which made me very suspicious. I should have put a hold on it while I sought an expert for help in identifying it.

Most of the surviving examples of furniture from this period are in museums. Fortunately, there were a number of folks with the foresight to buy and preserve some of the remaining items left over from these early days of our country. There are a few pieces in private hands which aren't as easy to look at as those in museums.

The furniture of this period generally is bulky and heavy; yet, there is a grace about it which must be seen to be appreciated. From the Jacobean period, we can see the press cupboard or court cupboard, looking elaborate and Medieval at the same time; there are heavily carved boxes, called Hadley chests, and the great refractory tables, not delicate but graceful for their size. And, anyone who has read about antique furniture in the past few years has heard of the Carver chairs, both real and fake! More chairs began to appear through this period; there were both elaborately turned chairs and very sturdy ones with all rectangular parts; some of these were heavily carved, similar to the carved chests of the day.

If you scan reference books which show furniture of the Jacobean period, you will see other chests, benches, tables, and a few chairs. There are some very pretty chairs, such as the Bradford and Churchill chairs, both of the "Brewster" style. There are some items which I personally think are ugly. But, we must not forget where beauty lies! The Wainscot chair is, in my opinion, ugly, and looks very uncomfortable.

It is important to keep in mind that chairs, as we know them, are a fairly recent piece of furniture. Through my research on early furniture, I have discovered that in the earliest inventories of estates, combined from Plymouth, Boston, Hartford, and New Haven, from 1633 to 1662, only 452 chairs in 271 estates were found, an average of less than two chairs per household. In some estates, no chairs at all were listed. Only important men had chairs to sit on; all others could use stools, benches, the floor, or stand!

Other than looking at examples of the Jacobean furniture which is safely tucked away in museums, there is another and sometimes delightful window into the past—paintings! In some early art work, you see pieces of furniture, usually the chair on which the subject was sitting. Obviously, that chair is as old as the painting, if not older. So, if the painting is dated, the piece of furniture also is dated.

Most of the earliest furniture made in the Colonies was of oak. Oak also was one of the favored woods used through that period in England. So, in order to determine whether a piece is American or

English, you may have to evaluate the wood, or rely on identifying the secondary woods, if there are any, since the cabinetwork was very similar.

I sincerely feel, while taking into account how very rare a piece of American Jacobean furniture would be in the market-place, you needn't worry about how to identify such a piece. If you are offered a piece of "period" Jacobean furniture on the open market today, I would assume it is a later English reproduction; but, find an expert to prove the point. If this happens, contact a reliable antiques dealer who deals in early period pieces, a museum curator in furniture, or a top auction gallery in a major city. Don't do as I did years ago and let it get away without finding out for sure; you'll never forgive yourself!

LATE 17th CENTURY: WILLIAM and MARY PERIOD. In 1689, William of Orange and his wife Mary, daughter of James II, became the King and Queen of England. William was from Holland; so, Dutch influences began showing up in furnishings of the court and the upper class. This, of course, filtered down through the gentry to the lower class, and, finally, to the New World. By the time the influence arrived on these shores, the 17th century was about over.

The William and Mary period was a nice change from the late deterioration of the square, bulky Jacobean oak pieces. The influence of not only the Dutch, but of the French, Italians, and Orientals was apparent. The furniture was smaller and more comfortable; there were more chairs and many were padded; and, everything was in better scale. Walnut was the predominant wood; hence, this period often is referred to as the "age of walnut", although many other woods were used as well, especially in the inlays or the "marquetry". High chests and highboys appeared; nicely shaped legs were designed and used; it was the beginning of the cabriole leg, which leads us into the Queen Anne period in the early 18th century.

William and Mary items can be found in the antiques market today; but, because of so many reproductions, you must be very careful. If you come upon something that early, in a price range which suits you, have an expert check the piece before you buy, unless the person selling is very trustworthy, with a good reputation, who will guarantee, in writing, that the item is a genuine, period piece. Have the understanding that if you find out otherwise, you can return the item and expect full reimbursement. Most pieces of this period which aren't in museum or private collections are very expensive and are being sold by pretty reliable antiques dealers; but, be careful anyway.

As you study the history of the monarchs and the furniture periods named after them, you will see that the periods live on long after the rulers. The best thing to happen to furniture designs from these early days was the fact that William married Mary; their short reign (1689–1702) sparked a great change as far as influencing the look of furniture and other furnishings. The furniture to come from this era is very pleasing, as far as I'm concerned. I know the whole evolution of furniture is important in order to understand the total scope of things; but, to me, the best designed furniture in America began with the early 18th century.

If you want to learn more about 17th century furniture in Colonial America, I would recommend that you visit as many well-known museum collections as possible. Every museum doesn't have items this early; before you make a long trek, only to be disappointed, call and ask a curator if they have anything from the Jacobean and William and Mary periods to show the public. There are quite a few restorations and museums in New England, the mid-Atlantic states, and near major cities throughout the United States which do have good examples of these periods of furniture. However, as I said, contact them first to be sure.

Your public library has a lot of information on its shelves about the furniture and furnishings of the 17th century. There are countless books and magazines where you can get bits of information about Jacobean furniture, the earliest of the early Colonial periods, and the William and Mary period, the beginning of civilized designs!

EARLY 18th CENTURY: QUEEN ANNE. After looking at the Jacobean and early William and Mary furniture, the designs of this period are very pleasant. Queen Anne, who was the sister of Queen Mary, and, therefore, a daughter of James II, only reigned from 1702 to 1714. But, the influence of the "Queen Anne" style of furniture still can be seen today, both in good reproduction, hand-crafted items, and in some of the stuff sold at furniture stores. The main influence, along with the continuation of the "age of walnut", was the introduction of the cyma (si ma) curve. This word is Greek and means wave. The curve is a double curve formed by the union of a concave line and a convex line, or we could say a simple double curve. Called the "line of beauty" by English painter and engraver, William Hogarth (1697–1764), some early Queen Anne chairs, using lots of cyma curves, are referred to as *Hogarth* chairs.

CYMA CURVE

This curve was a noticeable change from the straight lines of the preceding periods, and came into use in England about 1700. It reached our shores a few years later, and soon was very popular in the Colonies. This wonderful curve is the essence of Queen Anne design. It can be found on cabriole legs, crest rails, center splats, and often, rear posts of the chairs from this period. These lines also appear on tables and stands, day-beds and upholstered "sofas", mostly English, and on the legs of case pieces such as desks, chests of drawers and high cases. Nearly every piece of furniture from the Queen Anne period used this line, except the bedsteads. The cyma curve didn't appear on the feet of bedsteads until the following period, Chippendale, about 1760 in America.

Small tables or tea tables became popular because of the new habit of tea drinking. People started collecting china; so, china cabinets were designed, using the cyma curve on the feet. There were lots of changes during the Queen Anne period, most of them for the better!

During the early years of King George I's reign (1714–1727), there were still more changes in furniture designs and styles. George I was followed by George II (1727–1760); and, their reigns were during the period which we think of as Queen Anne. However, during the Georgian period, from the death of Queen Anne in 1714 to the beginning of the Chippendale period, about 1750, the English slowly were altering the Queen Anne lines.

Mahogany was becoming more popular than walnut; and, due to the new wealth, more elaborate pieces of furniture started appearing. Animal details such as ball and claw, hooves, and lion's heads showed up on the better, more expensive pieces. This was especially true in England.

As for the Colonies, until the Chippendale period, walnut continued to be the wood of choice by many cabinetmakers. Exceptions mostly were confined to the larger cities. Also, local woods were beginning to show up in more and more pieces of furniture throughout the Queen Anne period in America. In New England, common items often were made of pine; there were lots of very large pine trees from which to choose wide boards. Maple, birch, and cherry, as well as other fruit woods like apple and pear, also were used. South of New England, woods such as poplar and gum were added to the list. By studying where certain woods grow, you often can pinpoint where a piece of furniture was made, especially the common items or country furniture. Through this period, the American city cabinetmaker used the woods which were the fad in England, plus local woods for secondary parts.

Their English counterparts used, as secondary woods, oak and Scots pine, which often is called deal. Actually, deal refers to a cut of wood, and to fir or pine, not to a specific tree. This English pine looks different from the American version; however, it is very hard to explain these differences with the written word, except to say the grain of the English pine is tighter, and it seems to have more and smaller knots. The best thing to do is look at an early English import; check out the secondary wood, such as on a drawer side; then, look at a known American piece with pine secondary wood and notice the difference. In some cases it's subtle; but, it is different. If you're learning how to identify American furniture, you need to be able to spot the English Scots pine.

Try to do the same thing with a known English piece which has oak as its secondary wood. You will see that the English oak and the American oak also have a different look; the English is a little tanner. And, most American pieces don't have oak as a secondary wood. In many cases, learning to identify secondary woods is nearly as important as identifying the major wood, especially in the early Queen Anne pieces made of walnut.

Sometimes, the American and English are very difficult to tell apart; and, it does make a difference. Watch what happens at an auction to an American Queen Anne piece, if you want to see why you need to know the difference! For many, knowing how to identify an American Queen Anne piece may never be important. However, if you buy antique furniture, you never know when this information may be needed. It also is sometimes very difficult to tell walnut from mahogany; and, since the earlier Queen Anne pieces were of walnut, and the later ones sometimes of mahogany, you may want to try to learn how to tell these two woods apart. I've been wrong a few times; so, when I'm in doubt, I ask others to help or find a lab which can test the wood so I can make a positive identification. You only get this involved when you feel you have an honest, early, period piece to identify!

Keep in mind, the cyma curve came in with the Queen Anne period; but, it continued to be used until the Victorian period in some pieces. So, just because a case piece has nice ogee feet doesn't make it period Queen Anne! It's more likely Chippendale or maybe later. There are many other factors beside design which establish the age of an item. The wood, both major and secondary, the hardware, especially if it's original, and the construction are all important. On case pieces, drawer dovetails often are a good place to look for clues as to age. The earlier drawers had rather large dovetails compared to those on later drawers.

Tables and stands sometimes are hard to date. In many cases, all you have to go on are tool marks. Remember, the early tables were not held together with nails, screws, or "round" dowels. When something was needed to keep a joint together, it was a peg which wasn't round. The woodworkers of the early days used square pegs,

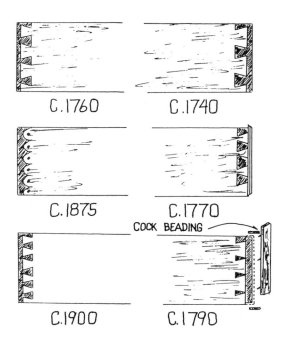

with the edges broken by a small hand plane; the peg was driven into a drilled hole. By doing it this way, they had a tighter joint. These pegs are easy to tell from the later round dowels.

One of the easiest Queen Anne items to identify is the chair. Most of these examples are from the later, rather than the earlier, part of the period. As a matter of fact, some "Queen Anne" chairs may date from the 19th century. A good example of later chairs comes from the Hudson River area of New York. There was a large Dutch settlement in this area; and, it seems they made a lot of these chairs. Often referred to as "country Queen Anne", these chairs generally are light in weight, have turned legs, sometimes with a single front stretcher, and have a nice crest rail and center splat. You can see the cyma curve in both the splat and the rail.

There are a lot of examples of early American country furniture which may have been made during the Queen Anne period; but, they don't have cabriole legs or use the cyma curve in any way. This is where you need to be able to date a piece by its hardware and/or construction, which, unfortunately, can't be taught on these pages. As always, if you really are interested in learning more about a style and especially about a period, you need to see the real thing.

Visit house restorations, museums, and any place where you feel you can see "right" items. Be careful of amateur restorations which could use fakes, reproductions, or pieces from the wrong periods, usually because they can't afford the real thing. You're better off not visiting places such as these than to be exposed to the wrong period when you are trying to learn. Read and look at the large selection of books on furniture in your library. Visit good antiques shows, particularly ones that have dealers who carry "top of the line", period items. Of course, be sure these dealers are showing "right" period pieces. Many times, you will see mostly English pieces at some of the antiques shows; that's all right, because by looking at the English furniture, and remembering what I've told you here and what you've learned in other places about American ones, you'll be able to see the differences.

I've seen lots of Queen Anne styled furniture being sold as "Centennial". Often, these pieces are reproductions made in the early 20th century. You usually can tell the age of such an item by the tool marks. Generally, a piece from the 20th century will show power tool marks made by either a band saw or a table saw. If these aren't visible, look for power planner marks which show up as a series of parallel lines when looked at in a good cross light. A real "Centennial" item usually was made very much like the period piece, but often is a bit "neater" and "cleaner". Also, you should see signs of hand tools.

When you get into this type of identification, such as, is it of the period, Centennial, or a 20th century reproduction, you need an expert. If you can't decide on your own, find a knowledgeable appraiser or antiques dealer, who knows period furniture, and hire this person to identify any item which is priced at period Queen Anne prices. If you are thinking of buying a piece of furniture which is supposed to be Queen Anne from an antiques dealer, have the dealer put in writing all of the pertinent information, with the understanding that you may return it for full refund if you find out later that it isn't what it was supposed to be. Don't buy a valuable, period, piece of furniture without a guarantee from the seller, unless you are buying privately; then, you need to take an expert with you. It's better to hire a professional than to buy an over-priced reproduction or fake!

The Queen Anne period continued in the Colonies long after Thomas Chippendale had made his mark in England, about 1749, as well as after his book *The Gentleman and Cabinetmaker's Director* was published. Even after the new Chippendale styles started showing up in the homes of the wealthy in the American cities, the country cabinetmakers continued the "old" styles for several more years. All of this just adds to our difficulties in dating such early pieces which is further proof that you can't know too much about what you're interested in, especially if your interest is in early furniture.

MID and LATE 18th CENTURY: THE AGE of MAHOGANY. With the lines of the Queen Anne style being applied to nearly every piece of furniture on both sides of the Atlantic, and the addition of the Georgian influence was keeping these lines from becoming boring, there suddenly appeared a "new boy in town", Thomas Chippendale (1718–1779). Chippendale worked with his father, who, it is believed, was a cabinetmaker and wood-carver. The younger Chippendale went into business for himself in 1749 in London. His early pieces of furniture were copies from the Georgian period and made of walnut, in keeping with the fad of the day. However, he soon started altering designs and adding his own tastes. A lot of his work was taken from people such as Robert Adam, who was a master designer and architect. Chippendale not only "borrowed" from the Queen Anne and Georgian periods, but also from Gothic architecture, and applied these designs to his furniture. In addition, he used a lot of ideas from Chinese and French designers.

He had the facility to borrow, improve upon, and apply other designs and lines to form his own, nearly unique, style. He was so good at this that by 1754, only five years after he had set up his own cabinet shop, he wrote and had published his book *The Gentlemen and Cabinet Maker's Director*, soon referred to as the *Director*.

This book was not a catalog showing items on hand, but, instead, was a reference work. It offered designs for prospective customers to look at and choose from. Of course, other cabinetmakers of the day, in the Colonies, England, and Europe, who made and sold furniture, also could get a copy; and, that they did. Soon, nearly everything was made in Chippendale's style; and, it came to be known as the Chippendale period or, the *Age of Mahogany.* Until now, all furniture periods had taken their names from the kings or queens of their day; Chippendale was the first private person to have a period named after him.

He was very fond of mahogany; and, by the time the *Director* was published, that was the main wood he was recommending in the furniture he both designed and made. Chippendale was a good cabinet-maker and had capable men working for him. Because of this, he was able to command high prices from very wealthy people. But, more than the items he made, Chippendale is remembered for his designs. There were other designers and makers of furniture during his "reign"; but, none left such a lasting mark on the furniture to be manufactured in the future.

Chippendale's influence in the Colonies is very evident; just visit any good museum! Every major city had fine cabinetmakers; and, I doubt that any of them were able to avoid making furniture of the Chippendale style. One of the most notable hubs of Chippendale furniture manufacture was Philadelphia, Pennsylvania. It was one of the centers of wealth, where elaborate pieces of furniture were made in fine mahogany, as well as with some local woods. As a matter of fact, there was so much activity in this area, that the designs coming out of here are called the *Philadelphia school.*

In England, Chippendale's designs were overlapped and succeeded by Adam, Hepplewhite, Sheraton, and others; but, the Chippendale style persisted in the Colonies well to the end of the 18th century. I would think one of the main reasons was "the war". There weren't a lot of good feelings and exchanging of ideas between England and the Colonies for quite some time after 1776!

After his death in 1779, Chippendale's son succeeded him in the business. He went into a partnership with Thomas Haig, which lasted until 1822. But, little more is known about the Chippendale family. I'm not sure what his son used for designs; but, there were so many new designers and furniture makers by then, that I would think he had to use whatever was most popular at the moment.

There were many more case pieces made during this than in the preceding periods. There were lots of drop front desks, many with enclosed book shelf tops; these pieces are called *secretaries.* As with most period pieces, they have gotten very expensive and have been copied and reproduced for years. So, again, be careful! This may be a good time to rely on an expert. Some drop front desks for sale today started life as secretaries; but, the tops were easily damaged and often removed.

Most of the better corner cupboards we see today were made between the first quarter of the 18th century and the early 19th century. I often get an argument with that statement; but, if you take the time to examine the really nice corner cupboards, you will see that I'm right. And, through those years, these items changed very little. The door panels, hardware, and moldings were all that changed with the periods in which they were made. After the mid-1800s, the construction, lines, and proportions weren't nearly as good as in the earlier pieces. There were a great number of corner cupboards made after those years; and, they still are being made. But, many of the nicest of these were made during the Chippendale period, mostly of good hard woods.

There were blanket chests and chests-of-drawers made during the Chippendale period, usually with either straight or ogee bracket feet. There were high chests, often with bracket feet, but occasionally with low cabriole legs. A high chest with cabriole legs is referred to as a *chest-on-frame*; and the word frame may be replaced by either "stand" or "table". Also, there were chests-on-chests, usually on bracket feet. The above-mentioned items generally were made of a local hardwood or mahogany, depending upon where they were made and for whom. More mahogany was used in the larger, wealthier cities than in country cabinet shops.

Highboys, which are chests of drawers on a base with drawers, and on high legs, were made through all of the periods I've covered. But, many more were made during the Chippendale period. Because of this, many of the ones you see for sale are late Queen Anne or Chippendale. The earliest highboys had turned legs, stretchers, and flat tops; next, came the cabriole legs, first with flat tops; then, by about mid-century, the scroll top examples appeared. Highboys were made until about the end of the 1700s.

Tables are a little confusing through this period. There are many examples of tri-pod tables, ranging in size from the small candlestand to the large tea table. Most of the larger stands or tables had tilting tops. There are quite a few drop-leaf tables of the Chippendale period; but, there are not many tables which primarily were made for dining as we think of such items today. Later in the century, as Adam, Hepplewhite, and others began to influence designs more, dining tables started appearing. The drop-leaf tables of the Chippendale period could be used in other than the dining-room, as could the English sideboard tables and the large, round, tilt-top tables.

Of the tables mentioned here, the earlier examples usually were of walnut, while the later ones may have been made of mahogany, particularly the higher styled examples.

As with Queen Anne, so many of the Chippendale designs have been used over and over, and still are being used. They are used for reproductions; and, distorted ideas of the Chippendale style can be seen in furniture stores where mass-produced items are for sale.

Finding a truly period piece of American Chippendale furniture for sale today isn't impossible, nor is it easy. What you often will find is a Centennial piece or a good reproduction. In most cases, Chippendale furniture is very pleasant to look at and fairly comfortable. Although the cyma curve often was used in his designs, there were a lot more straight lines than in the preceding period. On chairs, the cabriole leg, as well as straight legs, were used. The ball and claw foot can be seen, but only on the cabriole leg. There are a lot of general Chippendale lines; but, because he was so good at copying other designs, and since so many people used his *Director* from which to build furniture, it is difficult to make any definite statements about what to watch for when looking for a period piece of Chippendale furniture. There's the cabriole leg, also used in other periods, the *ogee* foot, also used by others, and, of course, mahogany. However, mahogany was used before and after the Chippendale period.

Another problem is that walnut was very plentiful on these shores and also was used in a great number of the Chippendale designed pieces. An added problem is that walnut and mahogany, each with an old dirty finish covering the wood, are very hard to tell apart. So, what we have to go on is a lot of "generally it's this way" statements, when trying to identify a Chippendale item. I will say, however, that if you aren't sure of yourself regarding any piece of period furniture, by all means, show it to an expert whom you trust.

Generally, Chippendale chairs have a plainer crest rail than Queen Anne chairs, although both may be in the shape of a cupid's bow. They both may have a center splat. A *ladder back,* not slat back, chair is Chippendale, at least in style. However, it may take an expert to decide whether it's a period or Centennial piece.

Some details to check when looking for a period Chippendale chair are mortise and tennon joints, since some, but not all, Centennial and most reproductions were made with dowels in the joints; take a good look at the underside of the seat. Look for tool marks and patina. Be sure the tools used to make the chair weren't modern, and that the patina didn't come out of a can!

Check glue blocks and corner blocks for signs of age. Corner blocks should be hand-formed and neither nailed nor screwed into place.

The same is true with glue blocks. These blocks were held in place by the glue. Glue was applied to both surfaces; then, the block was put into place and rubbed back and forth in the spot where it was to remain. Soon, friction made the rubbing difficult; at this point, the rubbing was stopped and the block left in place for the glue to dry. As a matter of fact, these glue blocks also are referred to as *rub blocks* by some cabinetmakers. Although the wood in a Chippendale chair most often was mahogany, other woods were used. Walnut was used occasionally; and, when a "country Chippendale" chair was painted, as many were, the wood often was maple, birch, or some other hardwood. As always, there's a lot to learn. Be careful!

Bedsteads of the Chippendale period often were very elaborate, especially in the wealthier homes. In this period, the high-post bedstead often had cabriole legs; but, in keeping with the period, some had heavy square legs. As wealth grew and homes became larger, the bedsteads became fancier. Many of them were of mahogany; however, woods such as maple and birch also were used, particularly in New England. The American high-posts usually were tapered; and, generally, fluting decorated the foot-posts.

As you most likely have concluded by now, this is not a period of furniture which is black and white as far as determining whether or not an item is authentic, Centennial, another period, reproduction, or fake. A Centennial piece or a reproduction item, both with a hundred years of use, could be very difficult for the novice or even the average collector to distinguish from the real thing. This is why you need a professional, who deals in and knows the period in which you are interested, to go with you when you are buying period furniture.

There are many reliable people who deal in period items; but, if you don't know and trust them, you still need assistance when looking. A good dealer who sells you a period piece will stand behind it, especially if you can prove it isn't as advertised; but, you have to know your stuff or have a very convincing assistant in order to prove something isn't what is was supposed to be.

I once heard a great adage "If you don't know the merchandise, know the merchant". I would add to that, "or know someone who does"!

LATE 18th CENTURY: ADAM, HEPPLEWHITE, SHERATON, and our early FEDERAL PERIOD. The most notable of the four Adam brothers was Robert (1728–1792). An architect, he and his brothers set up their business in London around 1758. They were employed by wealthy clients and became influential in helping to establish the "taste" of their day. When they designed a house, they did the whole thing, including the furniture and accessories—everything! They wanted all things to be in harmony with their architecture. They hired whomever they needed to do the work they wanted done. This included both Chippendale and Hepplewhite who made furniture for the Adam firm according to its designs and specifications. The Adam designs were much lighter than Chippendale and generally used straighter lines than Hepplewhite.

Not unlike today, everybody copied everyone else, with just enough changes to convince themselves they weren't copying. Therefore, you can see Adam influence in Chippendale, Hepplewhite, and later in Sheraton styles, designs they claimed as their own. But, after all, "there's nothing new under the sun," and all that! If it weren't for imaginative copying now and again, things might get pretty boring. That was true in the past, is true today, and will be true in the future.

The Adam brothers utilized a lot of mahogany in their early designs; but, later, they started to call for the use of a great deal of satinwood. Therefore, Chippendale's "age of mahogany" eventually became Adam's "age of satinwood." The Adam brothers weren't of much influence in our country, at least not directly. There weren't many of their designed items imported to these shores; and, there was no publication for our cabinetmakers to copy. So, here, the main Adam influence came from whatever appeared in Chippendale's *Director*, or from Hepplewhite's designs which had been influenced by Adam.

Items we see today that are supposed to be "period Adam" are either English, which would be rare, or made by an American cabinetmaker who got the design from a book, most likely *The Cabinet Maker and Upholsterer's Guide*, published by A. Hepplewhite & Co.

George Hepplewhite (?–1786) was a cabinetmaker in London around 1760. He was hired by the Adam brothers to build furniture; and, the best I can tell from my research, there are no known pieces which can be attributed to Hepplewhite's shop.

Hepplewhite-style furniture is much lighter-looking than the heavy pieces of Chippendale; and, instead of carving, his design relies on a lot of inlay with different colors of wood.

After his death, Hepplewhite's widow, Alice, in 1788, put together and published the *Guide* mentioned above. This trade catalog and the two later additions are the only clues we have on the subject of "Hepplewhite style." Utility, simplicity, and elegance are the key themes throughout the *Guide*. Apparently, the book's preface prepares the reader with the following statement, "to unite elegance and utility, and blend the useful with the agreeable."

After "the war," the Hepplewhite style became popular in America, and continued in vogue until about 1800 in the major cities. However, the straight tapered legs, seen on so many country stands and tables which may have been made well into the 19th century, often are referred to as "Hepplewhite style" legs. But, although they may be in Hepplewhite's style, that doesn't make them "period." A Hepplewhite period piece would be a lot more valuable than an item made in the Hepplewhite style. Again, this is where you need a lot of knowledge or the help of an expert in the field.

Late in the 18th century, still another man became famous for his furniture designs: Thomas Sheraton (1750–1806). Sheraton went to London around 1790 where he was a cabinetmaker, but in a very small way. He died in poverty. However, like some of his predecessors, his claim to fame was not his cabinetmaking, but the designs which he set forth in a three-part book. Most of his designs were dated between 1792 and 1794; so, anything of Sheraton's design would have to be dated after about 1792.

Unlike Chippendale's and Hepplewhite's books which basically advertised items they could make for a customer, Sheraton's book was for other cabinetmakers to use, a design book.

Sheraton-styled items are the last of the major English designs which were adopted in this country. Also, there are two Sheraton styles: early and late. When we think of good Sheraton design, most of us think of the early years; his later designs were strongly influenced by the French Empire style.

Much of this late style of furniture is on the market today. It can be identified by its heaviness of design, and bulkiness. Legs are fatter on both chairs and tables. Chests of drawers of the late Sheraton period usually have the largest drawer at the top of the chest, instead of at the bottom, as was customary. When you see that configuration, you are looking at either the end of late Sheraton or the beginning of French Empire; both are hard for my eyes to accept; as I've said before, there is no accounting for taste, including my own!

That pretty well takes care of the most influential furniture designers of the 18th century from aboard. But, what of American furniture designs of that period, our Federal period? This generally is thought of as after "the war", about 1780, to around 1830, when furniture of the higher style, not the country pieces, got bulky and massive; then, in general, good design gave way to mass-produced, poorly designed items, which many of us consider offensive; again, we're back to taste!

Through this period of furniture manufacture, especially in the larger cities, the English designers were the main influence. Although we weren't doing business with England through the war years, we also didn't have time to worry about "new" furniture designs. We were too busy with the "war effort." Any furniture which may have been made through that period would have been either in the Chippendale style or the Americanized version of his style.

After about 1780, we again were doing business with England; and, furniture was one of our imports. By now, the style of Hepplewhite had become dominant, strongly influenced by the Adam brothers. Our cabinetmakers not only had the books that Chippendale and Hepplewhite had published, they also had the actual furniture to copy, right off the boats!

As the years passed, our cabinetmakers had a new book, Sheraton's, with still more ideas. Although all of these books were strongly influenced by Robert Adam, they also were different enough to offer quite a variety for those with the means to hire good cabinetmakers. Add to these books the talent which was developing on our own shores, and you can see there was plenty from which to choose.

With all this information, there developed some wonderful formal and semi-formal furniture. In the early Federal period, there were some great cabinetmakers in Philadelphia, Baltimore, New York, Boston, and, of course, Newport, Rhode Island. This is not to say there weren't other "hot spots"; there were, in Salem, Massachusetts, New Brunswick, New Jersey, Charleston, South Carolina, and Connecticut. Actually, along most of the East Coast, there were good cabinetmakers turning out fine furniture.

As we look away from the wealth of the major cities, we still see much furniture being made by the country cabinetmakers. These craftsmen often used the same designs as their city counterparts, but altered them to suit the tools they had and their own individual talents. Usually, the country pieces weren't made of mahogany, as the city pieces often were; instead they were made from locally available hardwoods, such as walnut, cherry, and maple, and, sometimes, from softwoods like local pines, basswood, gum, and poplar.

The hardware on a country piece quite often is from an earlier design than the item it's on, mostly because hardware was difficult to come by, especially away from major cities; so, the cabinetmakers used whatever they had available, even if it wasn't the latest design. Of course, this can make dating some early country pieces very difficult, if not nearly impossible!

A very general policy to help date hardware follows. In the Queen Anne period, the predominant style was a drop handle, usually in the shape of a tear drop, which was held to the drawer by means of a thin wire, or *cotter pin* shaped device that went through the drawer and was bent over on the inside. Also, there was a small plate between the pull and the wood. The Chippendale period saw the use of *bail* pulls with *posts* which went through decorative brass plates and then through the drawer fronts. The posts were held in place with nuts on the insides of the drawers. To help confuse the collector, this type of bail and post hardware apparently first was used on late Queen Anne pieces. Also, there have been large numbers of reproduction hardware made in this popular style. The period hardware was made by hand, with hand-forged nuts and hand-cut threads. Most of the reproduction hardware, especially the later examples, are machine made; and, on close examination, you usually can tell the two apart.

Late in the Chippendale period, another type of hardware appeared. The bail still was held with posts, but the large back plate had disappeared. In its place, there were two small *rosettes*, with one post passing through each, and a nut on the inside of the drawer to keep it in place. This type of hardware overlapped the earlier style, and continued into the next period, especially on the country pieces.

The next general style was the oval plate which was used both on Hepplewhite and Sheraton pieces, as well as country items made throughout that time. During the last years of the 18th century, you may see other types of hardware on some Sheraton styled pieces. These could be either round or oval brass plates with either a round or oval handle attached at the top of the plate.

A very general rule of thumb is this: a small drop is Queen Anne, post and bail with a large back plate is early Chippendale, post and bail with rosettes is late Chippendale, oval plate with post and bail is Hepplewhite, and round plate with a handle attached at the top is

Sheraton. Please remember, this is very general; and, there are many, many exceptions. This just adds credence to my comments that when you are planning to invest in a period piece of furniture, have an expert examine and verify its authenticity for you.

There are so many extenuating factors when examining an expensive piece of furniture that, unless you are an expert in the field, you are asking for trouble when you try to determine the age of a period piece on your own. This is not quite as true with country items; but, the main factor here is price. It is one thing to pay a few hundred dollars for a simple country piece and make a mistake; it is a whole different ballgame to pay several thousand dollars for a "period" item, only to find out later that it isn't what you thought it was.

There have been a lot of reproductions, "Centennial" pieces, and out-and-out fakes made through the years. Many of them are in the high style of the period pieces; after all, that's where the big money is.

EARLY 19th CENTURY: AMERICAN DIRECTORY, DUNCAN PHYFE, and AMERICAN EMPIRE. As the 19th century began in America, furniture of the Hepplewhite and Sheraton influence still dominated the scene. However, people being what they are, the more affluent and the avant-garde of the day wanted something different. By now, the homes of the wealthy were beginning to look like "American" homes, slowly moving away from the "old" English influence which had prevailed; and, these homes needed "modern" furnishings. Concurrently, there were new designs and ideas coming out of France, due to the revolution which included the execution of Louis XIV, the power of "The Directory" (1795–1799), and Napoleon; lots of changes indeed!

The American Directory style is very limited, and hardly ever referred to; but, it is the style between late Sheraton and early Empire. The basic lines and construction are Sheraton in style, but with the French Empire touch instead of the Adam inspiration; this is what we call the American Directory period. About 1815, this style of furniture was being replaced by what generally is referred to as Empire, which prevailed and got heavier and worse as time went on, until about 1840. Then, Victorian was the "new" style. By this time, the industrial revolution was taking hold.

Factories were turning out semi-mass-produced furniture, and then mass-produced furniture. Deterioration of construction and design were rampant. The era of fine furniture was over. Some handmade items still were being turned out in country workshops; and, a lot of these pieces looked very much like their earlier counterparts, except for hardware. Many "country" items in antiques shops today were made during the period when Empire and Victorian were being produced in the cities. More on this later; now, let's get back to the early 1800s.

The new wealth and the new American homes called for new American furniture. There were several good cabinetmakers working by then; but, many of them still were making things in the "old" styles.

Duncan Phyfe (1768–1854) was one of the new wave of cabinetmakers who had a great deal of influence from about 1800 to 1825. During this time, he copied Sheraton's styles, with a bit of Adam influence, while keeping his final product light and clean-looking; his furniture became very popular among the wealthy. He was born in Inverness, Scotland. His family moved to Albany, New York, where young Phyfe was apprenticed as a cabinetmaker. In 1792, he moved to where the "big" money was, New York City, and opened his own cabinet shop. Around 1793, he changed his name from *"Fife"*, the old family spelling, to *"Phyfe,"* as we know it today.

Phyfe was one of the first American cabinetmakers to use factory-type manufacturing. At one point, he had over one hundred woodworkers and carvers working for him—not a small operation in those days! While Phyfe did not design furniture, he was very good at taking what was in vogue, improving upon it, and, therefore, pleasing his wealthy buyers.

By about 1825, tastes were changing again. The delicate legs of the Sheraton-style tables, chests, sofas, etc. were giving way to the heavy, massive claw feet of the French Empire which was coming into favor. Being a businessman, and running a cabinet shop with many employees, Phyfe knew he either had to change with the flow or be out of favor, and, therefore, out of business. Also, it didn't hurt matters that John Jacob Astor liked Phyfe's furniture. He helped popularize Phyfe and helped make him one of the "in" cabinetmakers of New York City.

Mahogany was one of the major woods used by Phyfe, as well as by a number of the other cabinetmakers of the period; and, there were many. Boston, Baltimore, Philadelphia, and New York City were "hot spots" for the new designs coming out of England and France. There still was some English influence in American designs; and the English were being influenced by the French!

This explains why French Empire crept into American furniture styles. Although there were many good cabinet shops in operation in the early 1800s, Phyfe got, and still gets, most of the "press". Some of the other cabinetmakers used a lot more veneer than Phyfe; and, most of them, including Phyfe, relied a great deal on carving to create their designs. By the end of the first quarter of the 19th century, most of the city cabinetmakers, from Boston to Baltimore, who had been copying Sheraton, were slowly moving into the heavier Empire style.

One of the reasons Phyfe is so well remembered as a major furniture influence of this period is because he consistently copied the best designers of his day, and applied their lines to his furniture, adding his own touch. His shop turned out fine furniture, using the best materials and finest craftsmanship. Although I personally don't like the high styled furniture after about 1810 or so, I certainly must agree that most of the furniture from Phyfe's shop during this time was very well made.

In the opinions of many, he was the last major maker of American furniture with "good taste"; major is the key word here. There were many "pockets" of cabinetmakers turning out some very nice items during and after Phyfe's "reign". This is especially true through the rural areas of New England, central and western New York, and Pennsylvania, and in the Midwest, notably Ohio. There also were groups, such as the Amish and Shakers, who weren't terribly influence by the designs coming out of France.

There was a lot of "Americanized" Sheraton and early Empire furniture being made all along the East Coast; but, as the American population moved west to "new" territory, their furniture styles didn't change very much at first. There are examples of cupboards, tables, chests, etc. which look much earlier than they are, mostly because it took so long for the effect of new styles to travel westward. Another factor may be that these folks had other things to worry about than what the latest furniture styles were; just to have simple, functional pieces was enough at the time. Of course, as cities were established, and started to grow throughout the Midwest, Eastern styles began to catch on. However, they never were quite the same as the "latest" in New York City or Philadelphia.

Now, a bit about American Empire. American Empire styled furniture basically used designs based upon English and French Empire lines. Late Sheraton gave way to the *Neo-classic* of the day. These "new" styles were, in reality, the revival of earlier Greek, Roman, and Egyptian lines. Everything was large and ornate. There was a lot of attention paid to heavy carving of claws and animal heads. There also was a lot of brass, and large mirrors. The furniture was rectangular, massive, and excessive, using rich woods such as mahogany, rosewood, and ebony. Sphinxes, swags, and festoons were in gilt. Much of Duncan Phyfe's late work shows this Empire influence.

From about 1820 to 1840, almost all of the "new" furniture and furnishings in or near the major cities was of the Empire influence. The industrial revolution was picking up speed and those with wealth wanted to show off. This they did with massive pieces of furniture, much of it now factory made. There was no regard for taste—just big and showy! The deteriation of good taste had set in. The only redeeming features about some of this late American Empire furniture were the use of beautiful woods and the fine workmanship found in most of these items.

By about 1840, the influence of Queen Victoria had worked its way to the American shores. With it came "new" designs for furniture, and the end of the Empire period in America. However, Empire-styled furniture was made for several years into the Victorian period. I will talk about Victorian later.

What do you look for when you check out pieces of the styles I've just described? First of all, American Directory and American Empire weren't reproduced or copied much until the late 1800s and into the early 1900s. Generally, these late items are easy to pick out from the originals; they are mostly factory-made and usually weren't made as fakes. Because of this, they are easy to spot by nearly anyone with the least bit of knowledge about tool marks and late construction. Most of these copies were made for an effect, or so someone could decorate in an earlier scheme. The Directory pieces were so few, and so close in feeling to Sheraton, that they weren't copied much.

What you need to watch for with this period are pieces from England, and sometimes France. Most of the imported items can be identified by the use of different types of wood than the American examples. Also, the lines are a little different. This is another area where you may need an expert with you when you are planning to buy. You should examine known American examples, and become acquainted with the woods, construction, general lines, and finishes before you buy on your own; and, even then, it helps to have a professional with you, or at least trust the person from whom you are buying.

Most of the copies and fakes through this period of time were of the Duncan Phyfe style; and, a lot of his pieces were copied. You often will see a piece of furniture tagged "centennial" or "turn-of-the-century" at antiques shows and in shops; these are the pieces to be careful of! A "centennial" tag usually is on Queen Anne or Chippendale styled pieces.

When you see a "turn-of-the-century" tag on a piece of furniture, often it is little more than used furniture; and, if you look around, you may find the same piece, or something very similar, in a used furniture store for a lot less money. I know that something made around 1900 could be over 90 years old; however, that doesn't make it an antique, not even close, not when we are talking about good furniture! Even though that tag rarely appears on furniture at quality shops, I do see it more and more on pieces in "antiques centers", outdoor shows, and, sadly, even occasionally, at an indoor antiques show. It distresses me; there is a place and a market for these items, but not at antiques shows or in shops.

Duncan Phyfe styled pieces seem to show up a lot with this "turn-of-the-century" title, especially dining chairs and tables. From my observations, many of these pieces are not turn-of-the-century, but were made after World War II. With the new prosperity after the war came an increase in new homes which, of course, led to a need for new furniture. The Victorian items owned by the parents of these young buyers weren't what they wanted for themselves; the *Danish modern* influence hadn't filtered to this group yet; and, Queen Anne and Chippendale styles were a little too "rich" looking for most of their modest homes. So, these new furniture buyers who were looking for something "traditional" for their diningrooms leaned toward Duncan Phyfe furniture. It was relatively light in appearance; factories could turn it out rather quickly and inexpensively; and, it was fancy enough to impress new neighbors and the older family members who would visit for Thanksgiving, Christmas, and other important holidays.

Much of this furniture stayed in good shape, since most families didn't use their diningrooms every day, unlike those families on television programs. Only used on special occasions and being well cared for has kept most of these pieces looking pretty good.

Duncan Phyfe period pieces of furniture generally were made of nice-looking mahogany with excellent craftsmanship. By contrast, the copies often were made with "veneer-grade" mahogany plywood tops, and glued up pedestal bases; usually a pedestal would have four legs. These bases generally were made of some type of hardwood, stained to look like mahogany, although much redder in color than real mahogany. Often, these later tables have markings on the bottom of the top. The marks may be the manufacturer's name or a stock number, certainly not something you would expect to see on the underside of an early table. Also, while looking at the bottom of the top, if the piece is late, you will notice the graining of plywood, or a secondary veneer covering the core wood of the top; again, this is not something you'd see on an early table.

As for the Phyfe chairs that went with these reproduction tables, the center splat often was shaped like a lyre or some other intricate design. It's front surface had good mahogany veneer over a core wood, often with a backing of another piece of veneer. This is very general; and, there are exceptions; but, this is what you usually see on these late chairs. Often the back and legs are mahogany; but, the frame of the covered seat is another wood. Turn the chair over; and, if it's a late one, you should be able to tell by the modern saw marks, screws, stain, and glue which will be apparent. If it's an early example, not only will it show age; but, also, you will notice some hand-saw marks, hide glue, flat-ended screws, and other evidence of an early piece.

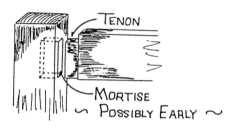

TENON

MORTISE
~ POSSIBLY EARLY ~

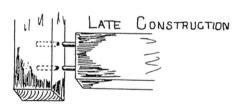

LATE CONSTRUCTION

If possible, look at a joint. The period pieces were assembled with mortise and tenon joints while copies were put together with dowels. Since dowel joints became popular during the industrial revolution, and generally were being used by the mid-Victorian period, you can't tell if the Phyfe styled items are turn-of-the-century or post World War II; but, since there were so many pieces of this style made from the late 1940s onward, I'd suspect them unless I could see something proving otherwise. Without proof of some sort, it's very difficult to date many pieces of furniture made after about 1870. If you study examples from the earliest years of machinery, you can see how primitive some of these early machines were. The furniture joints aren't too good; smaller and smaller pieces of wood were used, being glued up by machinery to get the size required for a piece of furniture. Wood grains weren't matched; veneer became thinner; and, as I mentioned earlier, dowel joints replaced mortise and tenons.

In the construction of drawers, machine-cut dovetails replaced hand work; bottoms were much thinner and weren't chamfered to fit into grooves, but were machine cut to fit. Add all of this information to the deterioration of good design and you should be able to tell a copy from a period piece.

Like the early periods, if you are looking for a real Duncan Phyfe, Empire, or Victorian piece, learn as much as you can about the style in which you are interested; and, if you're still confused, pay an expert to advise you with your purchase; this is always money well invested.

Keep in mind that well-made reproductions often are good buys, however, only if you pay less than a period piece would cost. Reproductions of a given period could have been made at any time from the years of the end of the period onward. Good reproductions were made as closely as possible in all aspects to the period pieces; the design, wood, hardware, finish, and even the type of glue should be the same as the originals. On the other hand, copies are easy to spot; they were made with whatever wood was available and with glue, hardware, design, and finish which may have resembled, but were not the same as, the originals.

MID 19th CENTURY: This is a very active period in the development of furniture design and construction. If you prefer Chippendale and Hepplewhite, you may feel this period saw the demise of furniture design and construction! In any case, a great deal happened. The most influential occurrence probably was the onslaught of the industrial revolution, considered to begin in the 1830s for the furniture industry in the United States. This period started the exodus of rural people to the cities, to the new factories, for the new money which they thought they would make. Cities grew around these factories, many of which were near rivers. With this newly found wealth came the desire for bigger and better things. This helped bring about many changes in the furniture industry, mostly the mass production of what many of us consider inferior home furnishings.

Changes in the manufacturing of furniture weren't all for the best, as far as aesthetics and construction were concerned. Not unlike a lot of things which are being made today, durability wasn't one of the factors in mind when many of these items were made; quantity was.

If you compare the joints and construction of preindustrial revolution furniture with many of the pieces made the "new" way, you'll see what I mean. As someone who has done a great amount of work on both types of furniture, I feel very strongly about this.

However, while the city furniture makers were trying to keep up with the new demand, a lot of furniture makers who worked in the country, or in the new territories west of the madness on the East Coast, were making pieces the way they had been taught by the "old timers". They knew how to use the hand tools which were available. In some cases, these rural cabinetmakers used a few of the power tools which were now in vogue, in addition to the hand tools they had been taught to use in the first place. Their pace and demands weren't as hectic as those of the city cabinetmakers; so, they were able to spend more time hand-making and fitting good joints. Their pride of craftsmanship hadn't been compromised by the need to make more money.

The rural cabinetmakers weren't the only ones who weren't too impressed with the "new" methods. There were others: the Shakers, Amish, and Community of True Inspiration, known today as the Amana Church Society or the Amana Colonies, are well recognized; and, there were others with whom we may not be as familiar. As you may have noticed, many of those who continued to make good, mostly hand-crafted furniture were religious groups. For most of these folks, quality was much more important than "new" and quantity. They were very slow to change; and, in some cases, chose to die out rather than change. I, among many others, am glad everyone didn't get vacuumed up into the madness for mass production which hit our shores in the second quarter of the 19th century.

Since the religious groups and rural cabinetmakers didn't make high style furniture, from this point on I'll refer to all of those furniture makers as "country", except when I'm talking about a specific group.

Although the country cabinetmakers used a lot of hand tools and old methods of construction, they weren't stupid. When they had access to power-milled lumber, they used it. This certainly made their lives a lot easier when it came to cutting lumber for furniture. Around 1850, circular saws powered by water wheels were being used. By this time, the choice, large trees which had been so plentiful were beginning to disappear. So, cabinetmakers had to start using trees for lumber which they would have passed up only a few years earlier. But, with the power saws, they were able to slice trees with large knots and gnarls and turn them into boards for lumber which eventually could be used in furniture.

Most of this inferior wood was used as backboards; but, a lot of it also was used for furniture that would be painted, especially in the last half of the 19th century, when a lot of "oak" graining was applied to kitchen and pantry cupboards. This generally is true with all of the rural cabinetmakers except some in religious groups who were a bit more discriminating, and usually used only the best woods available.

These country cabinetmakers did have access to "modern" hardware, and, in many cases, used it. Because of this mixture of old and new methods in furniture making from about 1830 on, dating country pieces sometimes is a real challenge; a lot of guess-work comes into play! The best way to attempt to date a piece of furniture is to look for the latest innovation on or in the piece. Often, this is the hardware: screws, nails, pulls, hinges, etc.

If you see a country cupboard which appears to be from the late 18th century or very early 1800s, but the nails are all of uniform shape, even though they have "square" heads, then you know the piece has to date from after the time these nails were available, regardless of the cabinetwork and the earlier look. Also, check the screws. You don't have to remove them to get some idea of their age. If the slots are "dead" center, you know they date from after the first quarter of the 19th century; and, since the "newest" in hardware showed up in rural cabinet shops later than in urban areas, you usually can count on the piece being later than it appears.

As for hinges, many country pieces have wrought iron "H" or "HL" hinges, and sometimes wrought strap or butt hinges. This holds for items made prior to about 1800 in country cabinet shops. After that time, and through much of the 1800s, cast iron butt hinges were used most of the time. But, again, you must be careful. If the country cabinetmaker didn't have access to, or money for, the "new" butt hinges, he'd continue to use wrought iron pieces many years after his counterparts in the city were using butt hinges. It isn't always easy to date a piece of country furniture!

AMISH: This religious group, some of whom arrived in the "new" world in the early 1700s, had a very hard time establishing their own "style" after they arrived. As most of you know, the arrival of early immigrants wasn't easy! After they were able to work off the debts they ran up getting here, they needed to work still longer in order to buy land or pay for a "land grant." However, once they got their land and started farming, then, and only then, could they worry about making nice furnishings; this they did!

Although "plain" people in general, they did have a colorful flair in their own way. Their furniture started out very plain; and, it mostly stayed that way. As the 19th century moved along, the Amish woodworkers used thinner woods and usually "modern" hardware, when they could get it.

After about 1850, much of their furniture was greatly influenced by Victorian designs. This continued through the 19th century, and well into the 20th, with very few changes. As with many country pieces through the Victorian period, it is very hard to really date them. Often the Amish, and some other country cabinetmakers, signed and dated their work; this is always something to look for when examining a country piece. But, be careful; make sure the date was put there by the maker, not someone one hundred years later! The Amish cabinetmakers had a good eye and were very good craftsmen; they still are. They used moldings and design tricks to make a piece look smaller if it was large, and to make a piece look larger if it was small.

As the rest of their neighbors converted to more power tools, and, when available, electricity, the Amish continued in their traditional ways, changing their designs little as they adapted Victorian lines, and using newer hardware when they chose to, but keeping the same construction methods which they had used for decades. Many of their case pieces had paneled sides, and often were painted red. They used moldings to add subtle decorative touches. However, the cabinetmakers needed to be careful with decoration; they were "told" to keep designs simple and plain. As I've said before, many of their pieces remained unchanged well into the 20th century. This makes dating their items a real challenge. You need to look for any indication of a date; and, then, hope that what you see isn't a replacement or part of an "updating".

Many of the earlier pieces of Amish furniture are of walnut, often with poplar as a secondary wood. Toward the end of the 1800s, oak became the wood to use, or at least to copy. Many of the pieces made during this period were grain painted to look like oak. By the early 20th century, a lot of these cabinetmakers had switched to oak, and were using the latest hardware, which was stamped out brass pulls, etc. Time caught up with the Amish; and, the demise of their furniture design followed. However, since they don't have electricity, they still use a lot of hand-powered tools. In most cases, these pieces of furniture are as well built as the earlier examples.

SHAKERS: What more can be said about this religious order of great craftspeople? Of course, crafts weren't their only claim to fame; but, that's what most of us remember them for. There have been scores of books and hundreds of articles written both by experts and would be experts; and, there is little I can add to these volumes except be very careful when buying a piece of furniture called Shaker! Just because an item is from New York, New England, Ohio, or Kentucky and is very plain doesn't make it Shaker. Your best protection here is to purchase Shaker furniture from a respected dealer or collector, with a written guarantee signed by the seller. I have seen so many pieces labeled "believed to be Shaker" or "purchased as Shaker", and even some called "Shaker" which I strongly feel were only simple country pieces mislabeled; rarely will the sellers of this furniture give you a written guarantee. The excuses offered often are worth the question just to watch the sellers try to get out of their statements!

There are far too many reproductions of Shaker furniture in the marketplace, and a lot of downright fakes, for most of us to buy a Shaker piece which isn't documented in some way. If not labeled during manufacture, as many of the later Shaker pieces were, then, you need a guarantee that the seller will take back the item for a full refund if you can prove it isn't Shaker. But, without an expert on the subject, proving a piece isn't Shaker may not be easy.

A lot of items which are Shaker don't look the part; and, many which look the part aren't! Be careful! Visit Shaker museums and any other museums which house Shaker pieces, to get a feeling for their things, especially their furniture. The furniture made by these people is very nice, usually quite plain, and most always well made; but, so are many of the reproductions. And, there are a lot of shops reproducing this nice furniture. Look through any magazine or other publication which caters to the antiques buyer; and, you will see catalogs offered; send for them; and, get some ideas of what is available. You soon will see how tricky it is to buy Shaker.

It's rough out there, folks, and getting rougher! But, with all of the museums, books, and very good dealers specializing in Shaker furniture who will guarantee their items, you can buy Shaker furniture or furnishings with some confidence, as long as you are cautious and very careful!

AMANA COLONIES and OTHER RELIGIOUS GROUPS: Most of these groups aren't very well known away from their main settlements. Like the Amish and Shakers, the Amana Colonists were people who came to the "New World" for religious freedom. All of them experienced grave hardships here, as well as in their homelands; but, persistence and hard work paid off for many. The Amana Colonists first settled in the Buffalo, New York area; but, as that region became crowded, they moved on to Iowa where today there are restored settlements. Most of these groups were self-sustaining, or as much so as possible. Many of them made their own fabrics, did their own tinsmithing and blacksmithing, made their own quilts, baskets, and other household goods, grew most of their own food, and made their own furniture. Again, like the Amish and Shakers, most of their furnishings were very plain and simple, partly from necessity andpartly for religious reasons. If you are interested in learning more about any of these groups, or in collecting their wonderful crafts and furniture, your best bet is to get books on the subject, either from your library or local book store; and, learn! Then, if time permits, track down settlements to visit, to see first-hand what their items look like and, in some cases, to buy samples of their crafts. Often, the new items made by these groups are very similar to those made years ago.

Since there isn't a lot of documentation on many of the various religious groups around the country who lived as the Amish and Amana Colonists did, your best protection is knowledge and a guarantee from the seller. Actually, this warning and general information about being careful should apply to any purchase you make which is expensive and of antique value.

LATE 19th CENTURY: VICTORIAN PERIOD: Much of the furniture made from about 1840 to 1900 is referred to as Victorian. Although separated by the Atlantic Ocean and different forms of government, the furniture designers of the States, and elsewhere, were highly influenced by what was going on in England. Queen Victoria (1837–1901) just happened to reign during a period of great changes, especially in the designs and construction of furniture. If good design started declining during the Empire period, its descent accelerated during Victoria's reign. However, we can't all afford period Chippendale; and, not everyone likes the same things.

Moreover, in spite of the design and construction decline in this period, there were some good and interesting pieces of furniture being made. And, it is too important a period in our furniture history to neglect.

There are three distinct periods within the Victorian era: early, from about 1840 to 1850; mid, from about 1850 to 1875; and late, from 1875 to about 1900. Here, I'm referring to the "city", or more formally made, pieces of furniture through much of the 1800s. As for the country made items from this period, there were few changes.

Toward the end of the Empire period, we blend into the Victorian; I use the word blend because, in the early years, it can be difficult to tell the two apart. In their search for something different, designers in these years were going back in time. About 1830, in the later Empire pieces, the Gothic style was revived. It wasn't very popular, but did carry over into some of the early pieces which we now call Victorian. Not all Victorian furniture is bad; nor is it all good. The early period had some very good construction and workmanship displayed in the furniture. The use of rosewood or mahogany in many of the items make the design, or lack of design, not too hard to take. It was a crazy period for furniture design; buyers couldn't make up their minds as to what they liked; so, many of the designers and makers of furniture mixed and matched designs from many different periods of time. There was revival after revival: Greek, Gothic, Turkish, Venetian, Egyptian, and Louis XV. Although eclectic in some respects, most of the designs were misinterpreted and unstudied. More often than not, some of the furniture to appear, especially in the later years of the Victorian period, contained a multitude of artistic offenses.

As the years went on, things got worse! Machinery and factories, combined with "tasteless taste", resulted in deterioration in both design and manufacture. By the mid 1800s, black walnut had replaced rosewood and mahogany as the most used wood. Marble tops were very popular, as were casters; both were used on stands, tables, and chests. With the advent of the jig saw came lots of scroll-work. This is most evident on an item called a *whatnot*, a shelf used to display glass, china, and ornaments. People now had enough money to collect "things"; and, the whatnot was a great place to display.

As carving machinery improved, the furniture makers couldn't leave a surface uncarved. Some of the items from this mid period seem to have carving over carving—very confusing to the eye, and much too busy to be pleasant!

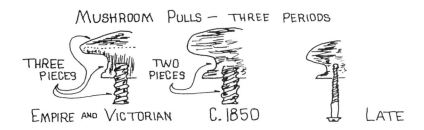

From the late Empire to the mid-Victorian periods, pulls for drawers were generally *mushroom shape.* The earliest were made of three pieces: the cap, the shank, and a threaded shaft which screwed into the front of a drawer. Next, the knobs became a bit smaller and were made of two pieces, the pull and a threaded shaft. The last mushroom designed pulls to be made, which still are made today, were one piece with a metal screw which went through the drawer from the inside, and was screwed into the knob.

By the mid-Victorian period, as machinery became better, woods used for backs, sides, and bottoms of drawers became thinner and thinner, as did the backboards of case pieces.

During the Empire and earliest Victorian periods, the cabinetmakers took pride in cutting very fine dovetails in drawers. By the mid-1800s, the dovetails were getting coarse and crude—no more pride? Too big of a hurry? In any case, this is one way of dating a piece. By about 1875, there was a machine which made a new type of dovetail. On a drawer side this new dovetail looked like a series of half circles with a dowel in the center of each. If you see this on a drawer side, you know the piece is 1875 or newer. Also, by the mid-1800s, wide pieces of wood no longer were used. Narrow pieces were glued up easily and cut.

Spool furniture generally dates from about 1820 to 1880. Around 1815, a new lathe was developed. Soon, some furniture makers were going crazy with it. At first, there was only a little spool work on certain pieces, then more and more as turners became better with the lathe. This spool furniture usually was made either of walnut or maple, the maple often stained to look like walnut. Most of it was country furniture rather than higher styled items. These spool turnings were used on chairs and tables, but mostly on bedsteads. The earliest bedstead headboards had joints which were cut on an angle. However, by about 1850, a method of bending strips of spool turnings was developed. So, any bent spool turnings you see are after this date.

Also, by the mid-1800s, doweled joints were replacing mortise and tenon, especially in the cities where doweling machines were available.

Through the mid and late Victorian periods, lots of things were going on in the furniture world; everyone was searching for something different, an identity! In New York City, from about 1840 to 1860, a prominent cabinetmaker named John H. Belter was very popular. His workmanship was considered the best. Although he worked in walnut and oak, his best work was in rosewood. To prevent shrinkage and to build strength into his pieces, he laminated several pieces of wood together, with the grains running perpendicular to each other. His work was very ornate, with lots of open fretwork.

From about 1830 to 1850, there were some pieces of German furniture imported into the States, called *Biedermeier* furniture. Biedermeier was not a cabinetmaker, but a character in a German humor magazine, Papa Biedermeier, who symbolized the common or "bourgeoisie". The furniture basically was a bad copy of French Empire.

The mid to late Victorian periods can't be mentioned without bringing up *Eastlake*. Sir Charles Locks Eastlake (1793–1865) tried to introduce some better designs into a deteriorating period. His designs were a combination of medieval outlines, ornamented with both Gothic and Japanese lines. This, coupled with the abilities of the new machinery, did lead to some changes in designs. At first, cherry was the principle wood used. It was embellished with metal, tiles, and conspicuous hardware. This furniture wasn't too good-looking to begin with; but, when the machine-equipped shops started mass-producing Eastlake furniture, any class or taste the originals may have had soon was lost in the distortions that followed.

With the exception of a few craftsmen who still did a lot of handwork, and weren't influenced by what was going on in the cities and outside of their own country, by the late 1800s, most furniture wasn't worth talking or writing about. One final bit of information on pieces which are called Victorian: *golden oak*. These items generally were made after 1900, and aren't really Victorian, although I often see them advertised as such.

Throughout this same period of time, there was a lot of "country" furniture being made just outside of the major cities and in the Midwest, which by now was getting pretty civilized. Although rarely referred to as Victorian, this furniture indeed was made during the Victorian period and was somewhat influenced by the new machinery and hardware. Examples are the Hitchcock chairs and the Hitchcock-type chairs and benches. Lambert Hitchcock (1795–1852) set up a factory to mass-produce furniture. He is credited with making *fancy chairs* from about 1826 to 1843. Most Hitchcock chairs were painted; however, there were some curly maple examples which never were painted, and were advertised accordingly. The first chairs he made, from 1826 to 1829, were stenciled on the back of the seat with *"L. Hitchcock, Hitchcocks-ville, Conn."*. From 1829 to 1843, they were marked, *"Hitchcock, Alford & Co., Hitchcocks-ville, Conn."*. In both cases, the word *"warranted"* also is on the seat; from 1843 until Hitchcock's death in 1852, the chairs were marked only *"Alford & Company"*. This type of chair became so popular through the mid-1880s that several makers started manufacturing them. Now, nearly any painted fancy chair with rosewood graining and a rush or cane seat is referred to as a Hitchcock! It has become a generic term.

There were lots of pieces of painted furniture being turned out of the country workshops from the early to the last quarter of the 19th century, much of it made during the Victorian period. You usually can pick out the earliest pieces by the hardware, construction, or marks on the wood.

In the hardware department, look at the screws, Screws with "off center" slots are handmade and usually date before about 1810; then, came the first machine-made screws. Those slots usually are near the center of the head, but the threads are fairly coarse and the ends flat, not pointed like the ones which followed in the late 1800s. Nails are another thing to check. In this period, most of the nails were machine cut, not forged, although forging went on long after machine-cut nails came into use. The main thing here is that the nails should be square-headed or cut, and that they haven't been disturbed or replaced.

Other hardware to look at are pulls and hinges, if they are present. Early in this period, most hinges were thick, cast iron butt types; these were replaced later by thin, steel hinges and in some cases, brass. The best way to tell if a pull, knob, or latch is original is to look for marks which would prove otherwise. As for dating this type of hardware, look at originals on authentic pieces of furniture from this period; then, look at reproductions. But, be careful; some good reproductions are hard to tell from the originals.

Construction often is a good way to date a piece of furniture. Remember, most of the time, a country piece has construction and hardware which may be 10 to 20 years behind a city-made piece. Look at dovetails and the thickness of the secondary woods, remembering what I mentioned earlier. Check the joints, recalling that dowels were beginning to show up, instead of mortise and tenons, in the mid to late 1800s. And, while looking at the construction, examine the tool marks in the wood, especially on the undersides of drawers, tops, and chair seats, as well as the insides of case pieces. If there are circular saw marks in the wood, it was cut after about 1850. Before that time, there should be straight lines made by a "pit saw". If the undersides are smooth, check for hand plane marks, a series of concave grooves, usually running with the grain of the wood. Watch out for power planer marks; they would indicate late 1800s or newer. These marks show up as a series of very close "washboard" marks running perpendicular to the grain. A small flashlight and a little knowledge can keep you from making a lot of mistakes when looking at furniture.

Many years ago, I bought a "nice cherry drop leaf table" from a little, old, grey-haired lady. She could see me only in the evening; the table was in a room with no lights; she had very little light in her home; and, she wanted to be paid in cash; *"I'm on Social Security you know."* Well, I trusted what she had told me about the table, since I couldn't see it very well. The next day, in my shop, I discovered I had purchased a stained birch drop leaf table. Not only that, it had had a lot of work done to it including one leaf which had been replaced with new wood! I had no recourse; I kept and finally resold the table. However, I now carry a small flashlight and am very cautious when conditions aren't favorable.

Knowing from whom you're buying also is often a big help. Because of the great interest in "antiques", there have been a lot of fake pieces made, trying to fill the demand. After a few years and a little abuse from a couple of owners, some of these pieces are hard to date.

TERMINOLOGY

CASE PIECES

In cabinetwork, the case is a box-like body which forms the shell of a piece of furniture. Case pieces, or case furniture, can be found in a great array of shapes and woods, ranging from the simple lap desk to the very elaborate highboy, and, from humble pine to the finest mahogany. A case piece can have several parts; the number of parts and what they are called depends upon the unit they make up.

BLANKET CHESTS:

The *blanket chest* most likely is the most important case piece. I'm sure the box was one of the first pieces of furniture ever made. As time went on, a drawer was added, then another, and another, until someone figured out a chest of drawers was probably rather convenient. Eventually, the lowly box evolved into the very elegant chest-on-chest, highboy, etc.

Since the Pilgrims most likely brought with them boxes containing their worldly prossessions, I'll start at about that time. These chests were made of oak. Many of the very earliest ones made in the "new" world also were made of oak. If you choose to go back that far, it is very hard to tell the English pieces from the ones made here. The oak is a little different; but, that is the major discrepancy. After awhile, the chests made here had more and more pine in them. Also, a chest with panels in the top often is English.

Some of the early oak chests had pine lids; when pine was used, it was a bit thicker than if oak had been used. The legs of the earliest chests were extensions of the stiles. A later addition was turned feet on the front only, with the rear legs being the ends of the stiles; then, later still, four turned legs appeared. Stile legs, however, were used on pieces for many more years, even after turned legs had become popular.

These early oak chests often were elaborately carved. Around 1670 to 1680, spindle ornaments were added. Sometimes a chest was decorated with both carving and spindles. At some point in the late

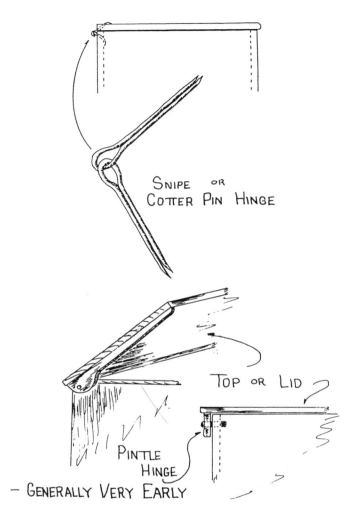

SNIPE OR
COTTER PIN HINGE

TOP OR LID

PINTLE
HINGE
— GENERALLY VERY EARLY

1600s, drawers were added to the box. These early New England blanket chests had two types of hinges: either *snipe*, or cotter pin hinges, or pins which went through the lid cleats and into the side of the chest, called *pintle* hinges. Also, some of these chest lids hung over the back about three or four inches. Then, when the lid was up, the overhang kept it from going back too far, a good design!

About 1690, the *Hadley chest*, also called the Connecticut chest, appeared. They first were discovered in the Hadley area of the Connecticut River Valley. These chests were of frame construction and highly carved all over the fronts with tulips and other motifs. They

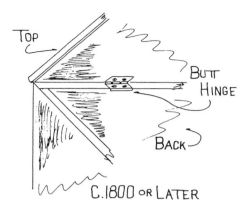

Top

Butt
Hinge

Back

C.1800 or Later

usually had a name or at least initials carved into either the center panel or the rail under the panels. Made mostly of oak, the lid, back, and inside wood of the drawers was pine. These chests often had one or two drawers.

Around 1700, the *six-board chest* became popular. These boxes sometimes had no feet, in which case they are called *sea chests*. Some had *bootjack* ends, while still others had *shoe* or *sleigh* feet. These blanket chests were much more primitive than the earlier boxes and usually just nailed together. Sometimes they had decoration, but often were very simple and plain.

Then there came the *chest over drawers*, often called a *New England blanket chest*. These boxes at times were very plain, while others were made to look like four-drawer chests of drawers. From this design came the chest of drawers in America; they just eliminated the chest storage area on the top and added two more drawers. Of course, blanket chests still were made for years after the chest of drawers evolved. Styles changed a little; and, around 1800 *butt* hinges were used, as well as snipes. By the 1820s or so, snipe hinges were used very rarely. But, do remember that snipe hinges can be bought today; and, they have been made constantly since their beginning. So, check other details besides hinges when trying to figure the age of a blanket chest. Snipe hinges are a good indication that a box is 18th century or older, but not proof.

While all of this was happening in the New England area, the Pennsylvania region was busy developing its own styles. While the English influence strongly dictated the styles of these New England blanket chests, the German settlers were the main influence on

STORAGE AREA ABOVE DRAWERS

C. 1800
NEW ENGLAND BLANKET CHEST
USUALLY PAINTED — SOMETIMES DECORATED

"6 BOARD" CHEST

USUALLY PAINTED — JUDGE AGE BY NAILS,
HARDWARE, TOOL MARKS, ETC.

chests made in the early settlements in Pennsylvania. By the 1770s, Germans made up about one third of the population of Pennsylvania. So, it is easy to see why they had such a strong influence. Their early blanket chests were painted and decorated in bright colors, mostly with religious symbols. As time went on, some of the symbols became stylized and lost a portion of their religious meaning.

A lot of these chests were painted with hearts; and, many of them had a young lady's initials or name and a date. Such pieces now are referred to as *dower chests*, blanket chests in which prospective brides kept things for their upcoming marriages. This type of chest, a *hope chest*, seems to appear in one fashion or another in most civilizations.

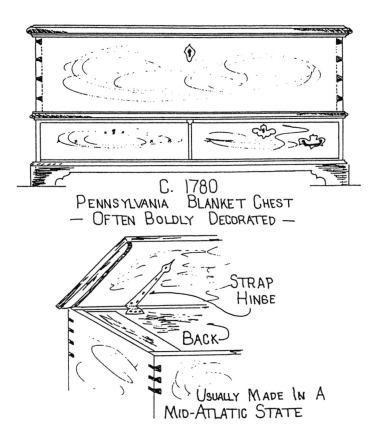

C. 1780
PENNSYLVANIA BLANKET CHEST
— OFTEN BOLDLY DECORATED —

STRAP HINGE

BACK

USUALLY MADE IN A
MID-ATLANTIC STATE

The Pennsylvania chests usually were made of poplar and occasionally of walnut. However, even the walnut ones often were painted. The construction of these blanket chests was either *dovetail* or the end boards were put into a *rabbet* in the front and rear boards; and, then nailed. The bottom usually was nailed on by fitting it inside and then nailing it into place with nails going through the front, rear, and end boards. Exceptions to this were the few examples which have shoe or sleigh feet; in these pieces, the bottom boards were nailed through the bottom into the chest front, side, and back boards.

Sometimes, these chests had no drawer; rarely one drawer, often two drawers, side by side, and occasionally three drawers, in a row. I don't know of any early Pennsylvania chests which had one drawer over another; that seems to only have occurred in the Connecticut or

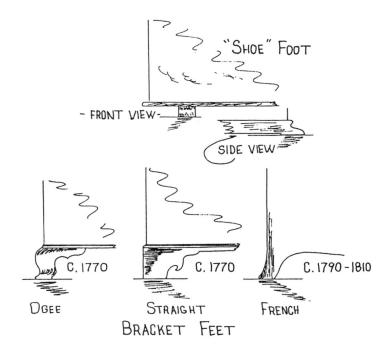

New England blanket chests. These Pennsylvania chests almost always had *strap* hinges prior to 1800. From about this time on, you may see some of these chests with butt hinges.

When these case pieces had a drawer(s) they also had a *waist molding* which was similar to the molding on the lid and base. The feet on such chests usually were either *straight* or *ogee brackets;* once in a while, you may find a *French bracket.*

Most of the chests I've been telling you about so far were made up to around 1800 to 1810. After this time, there were a few changes. By now, most cabinetmakers were spending their time and talent on chests of drawers; however, there still was a market for blanket chests. By 1820 to 1830, many of the chests from New England, New York, New Jersey, Pennsylvania, Ohio, and so on had started to look pretty much alike. The chest over drawers more or less stayed in the New England area; but, plain bracket feet were on chests from all over. Also, the *turned* or *bun* foot appeared in many areas. The turned foot had returned; but, it was a bit different from that on the 17th century New England chests.

Painting wasn't as symbolic as it once had been; instead, it had become more abstract. During the mid to late 18th century, you often could tell in which county of Pennsylvania a chest was made by the paint decoration. But, by the 19th century, that was difficult. As woodworkers and furniture painters moved around, they took their talents with them. So, by the mid-19th century, the best way to tell where a piece had been made was by the materials used. I have seen six-board chests in the Southwestern United States made of local woods; I've also seen frame and panel chests which were made in New Jersey. You no longer could tell where a piece was made just by its style.

There seem to have been very few blanket chests made after about 1870 until the 20th century when the hope chest came into vogue. If you are looking for a blanket chest or a dower/hope chest, it probably would be wise to buy as early a chest as you can find and afford, one that fits your life-style and decor. These boxes range from a couple hundred dollars to several thousand. On the bottom end of the price scale, you generally have just a box, usually with no feet or plain brackets. These work well for storing blankets, sweaters, etc. If you want something a bit fancier with nice paint, be careful. The blanket chests with good paint, maybe a name and date, usually cost a lot; and, when something becomes valuable, there often is someone around who's willing to make a plain piece appear to be something else.

A six-board chest can be converted into an expensive dower chest with the addition of bracket feet, strap hinges, and some fancy painting. If you are looking at one of these nice, colorful chests, be sure it is original. Check the underside; look for new feet, replaced moldings, and patches where butt hinges were; most of all, examine the paint. Look for evidence of a glazing or some other darkening agent over the paint to make it appear old.

A New England chest over drawers with boot-jack ends can be made a lot more expensive by cutting off the feet and adding molding and turned feet. Again, look at the underside; check for newly cut wood and maybe some stain where the ends may have been cut off. Changing the style, and therefore the value, of blanket chests isn't done a lot; but, it is done enough to look things over carefully before you buy. The thing to watch for most is the paint. Be careful!

Many blanket chests have a small compartment inside which is called a *till*; most tills have lids. And, some have "secret" drawers.

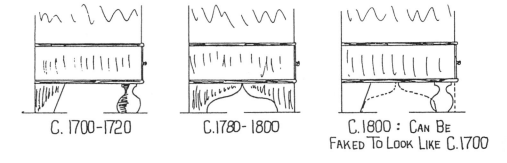

C. 1700-1720   C.1780-1800   C.1800 : Can Be
                                           Faked To Look Like C.1700

Since almost everyone knows where the secret drawer is and how to get to it, it's hard to refer to it as a secret drawer! Usually, the lid of the till is fitted into the upper corners of the front and back of the chest. It has dowels shaped into the ends to fit into two holes drilled into the case. The till front and bottom almost always are set into grooves, cut into the front and back boards of the chest. The front of the till fits into a *dado,* while the bottom fits into a *rabbet* or *rebate.* If there is a secret drawer, it is under a false bottom in the till; the front pulls up to expose the hidden drawer(s).

Nearly any home has a spot for a blanket chest. They can be used just for storage and hidden away someplace, or, if low enough, make a nice window seat or coffee table. A taller chest can be used as a server or a pleasant piece of furniture to look at, as well as for storage. No matter how you use your blanket chest, it always will be a practical piece of furniture. There is nothing as basic as a lidded box—just as useful today as in the 17th century!

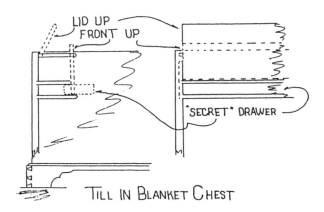

LID UP
FRONT UP

"SECRET" DRAWER

Till In Blanket Chest

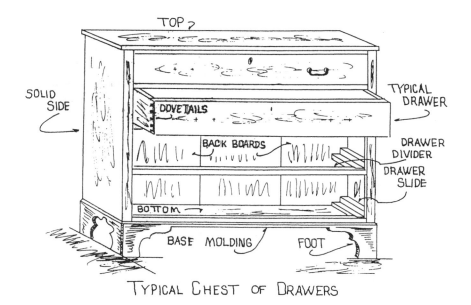

TOP ?

SOLID SIDE

DOVETAILS

BACK BOARDS

BOTTOM

TYPICAL DRAWER

DRAWER DIVIDER

DRAWER SLIDE

BASE MOLDING

FOOT

TYPICAL CHEST OF DRAWERS

CHESTS OF DRAWERS

The case of a *chest of drawers* consists of a top, sides, bottom, back-boards, feet, drawer dividers, and drawer slides.

The sides of some chests are not solid, but are called *panel ends* and are made up of stiles, rails and a panel. The sides on other chests may go to the floor; the bottom is cut out to form feet. This usually is a New England piece and fairly early.

Almost all chests of drawers of this era have four drawers; rarely will you see three, except in the later, small *cottage bureaus.* You may find some pieces with more drawers, usually of the Chippendale design and period.

Most chests of drawers from this time were made of hardwood, such as walnut in Pennsylvania, south to Virginia, into New Jersey, the lower tier of New York and southern New England, or cherry from southern New England to Virginia and points south and west to the Ohio valley; birch is usually from the states of New England. Maple also was used, generally in the same areas as cherry. Maple is a very hard wood to work using hand tools. Since the hardwoods were used over such a large area, the best way to determine where a case piece originates is to examine the *secondary woods.*

Secondary woods are the unexposed, or unseen, woods used in such places as bottoms, backboards, drawer slides, and drawer sides and bottoms. Sometimes, the drawer dividers may be of a secondary wood, and have a thin piece of hardwood glued to the front or exposed area. A very general rule when trying to place a piece by its secondary wood is: soft pine usually indicates New England while poplar is from New Jersey, Pennsylvania, Ohio, and southern New York to northern Virginia; hard grainy pine is usually southern. Cedar often is from eastern Pennsylvania, and yellow pine from central to southern New Jersey. This gives you some idea where the piece might be from; but when I say general, I mean very general.

I once worked on a case piece, a high chest, which had as the original secondary woods walnut, cherry, poplar, and pine. This piece was from southeastern Pennsylvania and completely original. The case was cherry, and dated to about 1790. It was what is called a transitional piece; the case and hardware were of the Chippendale influence while the feet were French brackets, which indicates Hepplewhite. As you can see, dating a piece of country furniture is made up of a lot of guess work, unless it was handed down through family members; even then, the facts seem to get distorted. The best you can do is to make an intelligent guess and live with it until someone can prove differently.

From the early part of this period you will find only a few softwood chests of drawers, usually of white pine from New England, or, once in a while, hard pine from the south, and an occasional pine or poplar chest from the Pennsylvania area. The real, country, softwood chests of drawers are more scarce than their hardwood counterparts, maybe because the softwood didn't hold up as well, or because country folks didn't have a need for such things; after all, what would a poor farm family put in a chest of drawers, if they had one, in 1780?

You will find more softwood chests of drawers dating from the 1820s onward than before this date; many of these were painted, often to look like a hard wood. Another pine chest of drawers you may see now and again is English, and dates from the last half of the 19th century. The best way to identify this chest is that most times it has two drawers, side by side, at the top; then, there are three drawers below, usually graduated with the largest on the bottom. The sides are solid wood, about ⅝ inches thick, thin by American standards, and generally are of more than one piece glued up and dovetailed at the bottom. There usually is a dust shelf, a partition of thin wood, between each drawer. Such chests almost always have turned feet. If you look at the wood closely, you will see that the knots are smaller than those of American pine. There is nothing wrong with these pieces; and, they usually are a lot less expensive than American chests of drawers; just know what you are buying; and, pay accordingly.

Drawers for chests of drawers throughout this era could give you an idea of age, as well as the talents of the cabinetmaker. You may see plain drawer fronts, drawers with lips, and drawers with cock beading. The plain drawer can be found all through this period. It is the easiest to make and very simple, like the woodworker who would have made it. The lip drawer coincides with the Chippendale period; and, the cock beading seems to have started in the last quarter of the 18th century.

Dovetails also tell a lot about the date of a piece; from the early pieces up to the mid 18th century, the dovetails were rather crude; next, they became finer and finer, very clean, and well done. Then, after the Sheraton and Empire periods, they were not as well done and evenly spaced. Finally, with the advent of water powered tools, you begin to see machine-made dovetails. And, around 1870–1880 the dowelled dovetail showed up.

HIGHBOYS, LOWBOYS, ETC.

The *highboy* is considered the ultimate chest of drawers. It has been called the last step in the evolution of the chest; and, it certainly is a fine example of a case piece. A highboy is a tall, two-section, chest of drawers. The base has a few small drawers, and stands on legs. The upper section has several large graduated drawers and usually a row of small drawers at the very top. The top itself may be flat, as with a country piece, or can be very elaborate, as in a more formal example.

A *lowboy* looks very much like the lower section of a highboy, and often is called a dressing table. Some fine, early cabinetmakers occasionally made a highboy and lowboy to match. Seeing a pair like this is not an every day event; however, they do exist.

A *tall chest* is a high chest of drawers with short feet. It is very similar to the *chest-on-chest* which really is two chests of drawers, one on top of the other. Highboys and tall chests both were made for storage; but, the tall chest was, and is, more practical since it has less wasted space.

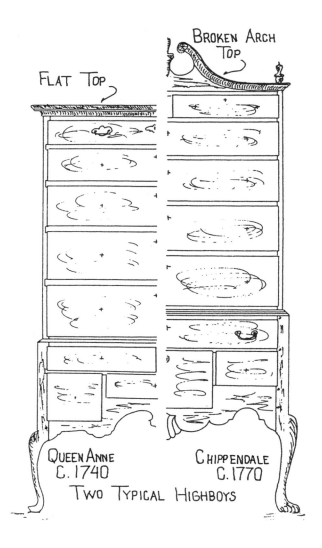

FLAT TOP

BROKEN ARCH TOP

QUEEN ANNE
C. 1740

CHIPPENDALE
C. 1770

TWO TYPICAL HIGHBOYS

Highboys, lowboys, and tall chests often were high-style or rather formal; however, there are a lot of country examples. The more formal pieces usually were mahogany or walnut. The country cases often were walnut, cherry, or figured maple such as bird's eye and/or tiger. Not as common were pieces made from pine or poplar; but, there are examples in these soft woods, most of which were painted. The hardwood cases usually were left in natural finishes; but, occasionally, they too were painted.

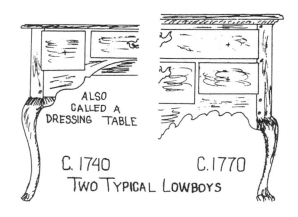

ALSO
CALLED A
DRESSING TABLE

C. 1740   C. 1770
TWO TYPICAL LOWBOYS

It seems that most high styled highboys, lowboys, and tall chests were made either in the Philadelphia or Boston areas, with some pieces from the southeastern section of New England; and, there were a few pieces made in the Virginia area. The periods in which most of these case pieces were made ranged from about 1700, the William and Mary period, to the early 1800s, the end of the Chippendale period. I have seen tall chests and highboys with inlay on the fronts of the stiles and drawers. Such inlay is typical of the Hepplewhite period, 1790-1810; however, all of the other construction and style of these pieces dates from the Chippendale period.

The tall chest and chest-on-chest didn't appear until late in the Queen Anne period, around 1750–1760; and, they continued to be made through the end of the Chippendale period.

There were, and still are, pieces made after the Chippendale period. But they usually are only copies of William and Mary, Queen Anne, or Chippendale. As with many other types of furniture, there were a lot of these pieces made for and during the 1876 Centennial. Most of these copies were done in the Chippendale style. Sometimes, it is very difficult to distinguish a period highboy from a Centennial one without the help of a professional. A lot of the Chippendale copies have veneered drawer fronts; and, often veneer was used in other areas, while most of the Chippendale period pieces were made without veneer. Also, you can tell a Centennial piece from a period one by examining the hardware. The early hardware is a bit cruder, although well done. If you are looking at one of these case pieces, check the dovetails in the case itself, top and bottom. If the piece is "of the period", the dovetails often are larger and cruder than those of a later copy.

When examining a piece, you also should watch for "reverse faking". Many years ago, I received a tall chest from a dealer to restore. It was a Centennial piece, covered with nice mahogany veneer, and having hardware from the 1870s which were copies of Chippendale pulls. The style was pure Chippendale except for the fancy grained veneer. I was to tighten the case, make the drawers work better, and refinish the piece. Someone had put a varnish stain over the whole case, inside and out, including the insides of the drawers, as well as the inside of the case. Because of this varnish, it was hard to see just what the inside of the case looked like, or even what kind of wood it was. I knew it was heavy; I had to move it from one place to another a couple of times! The first thing to catch my attention was the very wide, hand planed, backboards. They seemed rather early for a Centennial piece.

The day came when I was going to start working on it. Since the top molding was loose, I used a small ladder to get high enough to carefully remove that molding from the case. This put me a bit higher than the chest. While working on the molding, I noticed the dovetails were large and much cruder than I would expect to see on a piece dating from 1876. After I removed the moldings, I put the chest on its back to examine the bottom; it looked much earlier than the piece was supposed to be. Now, I was really curious. So, with paint remover, I cleaned away some of the varnish from the inside of a drawer front; it was walnut under the mahogany veneer! Then, I cleaned some of the inside of one of the case sides. It too was walnut! At a point near the bottom of a case side, the veneer was starting to peel. So, I removed some of it and found clean, good-looking walnut under the veneer. I talked with the dealer who owned the piece, and told her what I had found. We decided it would be better to have a period tall chest rather than a Centennial piece. I carefully removed all of that veneer—many hours later, I had found a period tall chest! Under the veneer on the drawer fronts were all of the marks from the original hardware! Someone had "modernized" that old piece of furniture for the Centennial; and it had come down through a few generations as a Centennial piece! Needless to say, the dealer was thrilled by my discovery! So, it pays to look at everything very carefully!

Whether the piece is high style or country, the area in which it was made can be guessed in a similar manner as with a chest of drawers. If the main wood is walnut, the piece most likely is from Pennsylvania; if it is maple of birch, it probably was made in the New England area. Also, if the main or secondary wood is pine, a New England origin is likely. Poplar probably would indicate Pennsylvania; cherry could be mid-Atlantic or southern. If the piece is made of mahogany, you will have to check the secondary wood to find its possible origin, since all of the mahogany wood was imported.

Finding good highboys for sale isn't as easy as finding chests of drawers; but, they are around and generally are rather expensive. However, if you want a lowboy, that is another story! There weren't that many lowboys made; and, they command high prices if they are right. Even a reproduction, copy, or fake, whatever you want to call it, usually brings a high price if it isn't too obvious that the piece is late. One of the things you must watch for with lowboys is reworked pieces. Check that the top isn't a replacement. Sometimes, the lowboy that you see started life as the bottom of a highboy!

Since lowboys are so rare, often one will bring as much, or more, than a nice highboy of the same style and period. If someone takes a country, medium priced, flat-top highboy and separates the upper section from the bottom, then puts a top made of the same wood on the bottom section, and next refinishes this as a unit, it is hard to see the difference between it and an authentic piece. And, by putting nice bracket feet and some molding on the bottom of the upper section of the highboy, it then becomes a chest of drawers. If the top of this upper section isn't suitable for a chest of drawers, it is no big deal to change it by adding different molding. By doing all of this, a medium-priced highboy can be turned into an expensive lowboy and a costly chest of drawers. And, if the work is done properly by a good woodworker, it is very hard to tell that the pieces aren't "right".

But, one thing that may be a giveaway with the chest of drawers is that many highboys have two or three small drawers at the very top, above the graduated larger ones, while most chests of drawers do not have such a row; so, if you see small drawers like this on a chest, examine the piece carefully, especially if you are thinking of buying it. The chest of drawers may be right; but, there is a chance that it once was the top of a highboy. If you see a piece you question, look at the underside, particularly the corner blocks, and the inside of the feet.

If the underside of the bottom has scratches, rub marks, and/or other indications that it once sat directly on another surface, and if the corner blocks look new, or newer than the rest of the piece, be careful. Look for new saw marks and raw edges on the foot cut-outs, as well as modern glue on the glue blocks.

Tall chests and chests-on-chests aren't as easy to fool around with; a tall chest is a tall chest; and, that's about it. A chest-on-chest could be converted to two chests of drawers; however, there would be little advantage to this type of conversion, unless one of the sections was somehow damaged, maybe in a fire. And, if this is the situation, saving one section makes sense. Again, the best way to tell is by examining everything very carefully.

As I mentioned earlier, lowboys also are referred to as dressing tables. Unlike highboys and tall chests, dressing tables stayed in vogue and were made well into the Victorian period. The dressing tables made after the Chippendale period can't really be called lowboys; they just don't look anything like what we think of as a lowboy, although they have basically the same configuration. Dressing tables were popular in the Sheraton, Empire, and Victorian periods. They served the same purpose as the lowboy, but really were quite different. Some of these were made of hardwood; but, many were painted and made from a mixture of soft and hard woods. Some of these later dressing tables work quite well as servers, if you find one you like and don't need as a dressing table.

Highboys, lowboys, and tall chests are not plentiful at reasonable prices; but, they are nice pieces of furniture, and can make a big difference in a bedroom, or in any room where you might have the need for good storage. Since these are expensive pieces, do be careful when buying one.

DESKS

Most likely, when someone says the word *desk*, the first thing to come to mind is the desk you have and/or use, whether it is your desk at home or in an office. However, there are a great number of different types of desks. Some may not fall into the case category; but, I'm going to talk about them anyway.

I would think it's safe to say that everyone reading this has gone to school; and, if you've been in school, you most likely used a desk of

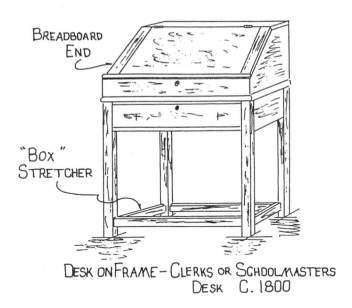

BREADBOARD
END

"BOX"
STRETCHER

DESK ON FRAME — CLERKS OR SCHOOLMASTERS
DESK C. 1800

some type. Depending upon your age and where you went to school, your desk could have been little more than a bench and table with a storage area under it, or a cast iron framework with enough wood bolted or screwed to it to make it a workable desk, neither of which are case pieces. But, both are desks.

I remember starting first grade in a rather advanced region in central New Jersey in the 1930s, where the desks were individual; the storage area and seat were hooked together somehow. In the middle of the school year, my family moved to a more rural part of Pennsylvania. The desks were more primitive; two or three of us sat on one bench and worked from one desk top. That was the last year for that school; but, those desks had been used since the mid-1800s! The next year, the desk I had was similar to the one I had used in New Jersey, and, was of Victorian vintage.

Another type of desk which really isn't a case piece is the *lap desk*. Basically, this was a portable desk which could be used almost anywhere. I gather they were used mostly by ladies. Some of these desks are quite elaborate with lots of inlay, not only of fancy woods, but also of ivory, mother of pearl, etc. The main wood used in most lap desks was mahogany. But, exotic woods such as teak, rosewood, ebony, zebra wood, and so on also were used. Some desks were veneered with bird's eye maple. Some were made of pine and grain

OFTEN· WITH A SMALL "GALLERY"

COUNTER DESK - C.1850
INSIDE MAY HAVE A SHELF, DRAWERS, OR NOTHING
USUALLY PAINTED OR GRAINED

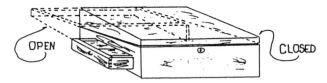

OPEN   CLOSED

TYPICAL LAP DESK - C.1840
OFTEN WITH OUTSIDE DRAWER - INSIDE FITTED
WITH INK WELLS, FELT COVERED WRITING AREA,
STORAGE FOR PENS AND POINTS, AND WRITING PAPER

painted. Many of them seem to be European or English in origin; and, most were made during the Empire and Victorian periods.

Still another desk which is more a box than a case piece is one called a *school-master's desk, clerk's desk,* or *desk-on frame.* This desk without the legs is called a *counter desk* and most likely was used in stores, mills, factories, or any place where a simple desk was needed and there was sufficient counter space. When looking at a desk-on-frame, be sure it isn't a counter desk with a new base. This is something which is done a lot. If it is, pay accordingly. Things to watch for are the wood on the desk and the base which should be the same; also, the color and wear of both should match.

Another desk of similar style is the type where the base is part of the whole unit. This also is called a desk-on-frame; but, you usually don't have to worry about whether the base is original to the top.

Desks of this style date from the late 17th century to the late Victorian period. A great number of the counter desks were country-made for country use; and, it is very hard to tell the age. As has been mentioned before, country woodworkers were usually a bit behind their city counterparts in their construction, often using hardware

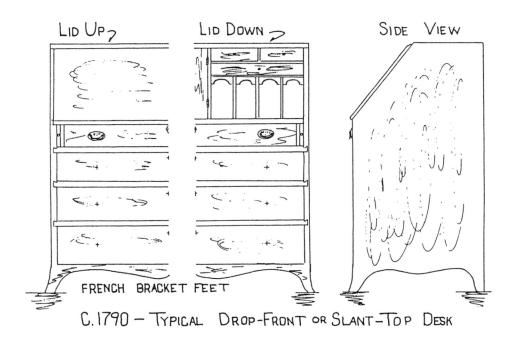

LID UP⁊   LID DOWN ⊃   SIDE VIEW

FRENCH BRACKET FEET

C. 1790 — TYPICAL DROP-FRONT OR SLANT-TOP DESK

and nails which had been around for some time; because of this, it is very hard to date an item such as a counter desk or a desk-on-frame, if it is country-made.

The desks which are case pieces started out basically as desks-on-frames with drop lids. The earlier examples, which were little more than boxes with lids, had the lids hinged in the back so they opened from the front; this required removing things from the working surface in order to get to the inside, or dumping everything on the floor behind the desk! Later, the lid was hinged at the lower front and opened from the top. Around the same time, or maybe a little earlier in some areas, you begin to see the *slant-front* or *drop-lid* desk which otherwise looks like a chest of drawers with a lid at the upper section. Usually, these desks had pigeon-holes, and later had lots of little drawers, including "secret" ones. Often the secret drawers were behind false fronts or other rather shallow drawers.

Slant-front desks with bookcases on their tops are called *secretaries*. These high desks have doors on the upper sections with *lights* (glass) or *blind* (solid panel). The earlier secretaries had panel doors; glass was scarce and therefore very expensive.

The styles, woods used, and methods of construction were about the same as those for chests of drawers of the same periods. The terminology for a desk is very similar to that for a chest of drawers.

Since slant-front desks are more valuable than chests of drawers, especially the simple country pieces, you must be alert when looking for a country desk. I have seen slant-front desks which started out as chests of drawers. It isn't an easy task; but, a skilled woodworker with a good imagination can take a chest of drawers apart, make some alterations, and put it back together as a slant-front desk. What you want to watch for here is a difference in the color of the woods on the lid and the case itself. Also, check the drawer construction and type of wood in the bottom drawers; and, compare them to the drawers inside the slant top area. You are not likely to run into one of these "conversions"; but, you should know they exist.

There is a full line of desk styles from which to choose in the antique furniture market, ranging from the very simple, early boxes to the late Victorian secretaries, and almost any style you want in between! There have been a lot of reproduction slant-front desks made through the years, including several during the American Centennial period. Most of these copies were made in the Chippendale style with bracket feet. They weren't really produced as fakes; it's just that the style was in vogue then. With a little knowledge of antique furniture, you usually can pick them out from the real thing. The best way to do this is to visit a museum or house restoration and examine a period desk. Then, when you see a Centennial piece, you should be able to tell the difference.

Desks usually were kept in the family for generations and often were "modernized" as styles changed, especially in the hardware department. I have worked on Chippendale period desks which had as many as five different types of hardware on them through the years, and a couple of desks which had the bracket feet removed at some point. In one case, very heavy castors were put on in place of the feet! So, when you look at a piece such as a desk, try to think of everything anyone could have done to it through the years; and, watch for changed hardware and replaced feet. Sometimes, a piece which has had minor changes is a good buy; if the case itself hasn't been altered, the hardware and feet, as well as the finish, can be corrected for a minimal cost, especially considering the price of a perfect piece which doesn't appear to have had anything done to it.

Secretaries should be examined carefully to be sure you aren't looking at a "marriage". A good woodworker could build a top for a slant-front desk, and match the woods and construction. Sometimes, this might be fake, while, other times, it may be a case where the owner wanted more space and had a new top made. In either event, if you are paying the price for a good secretary, be sure you are getting one. Check the back of the top section to be certain the wood, color, and construction are the same as the desk back. If the top section has drawers in it, which it may, make sure their construction is the same as that of the drawers in the lower section, especially the dovetails. Some of the very early tops didn't have drawers, just a lot of pigeon-holes. Later, solid panel doors were added to cover them; then, book shelves took the place of some of the pigeon-holes; and, finally, glass doors came into vogue.

As with chests of drawers, desks of the slant-front style were made of many different woods, and in several parts of the country. The same wood/area information applies to both types of case pieces. You will find some slant-front desks in pine or poplar, usually painted, often with great graining. But, most of them were made of hardwood. Many of the early examples of desks-on-frames were of softwood and painted; however, a lot of these have been refinished or repainted by now. You will see more counter desks and desks-on-frames than you will the higher styled slant-front desks. These simple boxes with lids have been made for a very long time; and, there were a great many more of them than the slant-front style or secretaries; so, for the person looking for a country desk, the desk-on-frame may be the best buy.

CLOCKS

So far, I have covered case pieces such as chests of drawers, desks, highboys, lowboys, and tall chests. Now, I will talk about a different type of case piece, but, nevertheless, a very important item: the clock, specifically, the tall case clock.

Before 1875, this type of clock was referred to as a *tall case clock*. A songwriter named Henry Clay Work published a song in that year entitled, *"Grandfather's Clock"*. Over 800,000 copies of the song sheet soon had been sold; and, tall case clocks became grandfather clocks to many people. I have not seen a copy of that music since I was in grade school; we had to sing it every time the music teacher would visit our class because she loved it. I don't remember loving that song as a child; however, now, I have a much better understanding of some of the phrases! In any case, I do not recall what the sheet music cover looked like; but, there is supposed to be a clock on it that looks a bit like a 1850 type *regulator* with a crudely painted moon face. Work supposedly had written the song long before it was published which may have something to do with the clock on the cover.

At any rate, the tall case clock as we know it today, fully enclosed, was being made from around 1680. Prior to that time, the clock works sat on a shelf, the pendulum swinging below; this type of clock is called a *wag-on-the-wall*. Around 1640, the short or bob pendulum was invented; but, it generally wasn't used until about 1675. The long pendulum was being used by 1680. From 1680 to 1700, the cases were very plain and simple. They sat flat on the floor without feet of any kind. Also, the hoods were plain. Around 1700 to 1710, pillars and bun feet, as well as other William and Mary features, appeared. Then came the Queen Anne period with arched, more finished tops; the pillars on the hoods were turned; and, most cases had feet, either bun, ball, or toward the end of the period, a few ogee brackets. The cyma curve had arrived! Around 1725, bonnets became more elaborate; and, the broken arch first appeared. From 1750 or so, styles really became elaborate and refined. This Chippendale period brought about scroll tops, carved finials, shell-carved and block-front doors, inlay, fluted pillars, etc.

Most of this early clock action was going on in England. There were a few clocks made in the Philadelphia and Boston areas from about 1730; but, not many. Most American tall case clocks were made between 1760 and 1840. Of course, there were tall case clocks made after 1840; but, the workmanship, style, and materials leave a lot to be desired.

Another type of tall case clock, which isn't so tall, is the *Grandmother clock*. It ranges in height from about 3 to 5½ feet and is rather scarce; it is so scarce, in fact, that there is some fakery with these short clocks. I have heard of some damaged tall case clocks being cut down and reworked to make them rare grandmother clocks. If you ever see a grandmother clock for sale, and are thinking of purchasing it, be sure it wasn't once a grandfather clock which had been badly damaged at some point.

Still another type of popular clock is the early *shelf clock*. Some of the makers of tall clocks also made shelf timepieces. In the early 1800s, a young clockmaker named Eli Terry started making shelf clocks by mass-production at the very low price of $15.00 each. Before this time, clocks were only for the wealthy. The Terry clocks were copied by many, including Seth Thomas, who had been an employee of Terry's. Thomas also became a famous clockmaker in his own right.

There were many clockmakers who made tall cases, as well as the clock works. Cases were made to fit a wag-on-the wall already owned by a family, sometimes brought from the "old country", other times purchased here. There were so many case makers, I wouldn't want to take the time to try to track down all of them. Also, a lot of cases were made by woodworkers other than clockmakers, which just adds to the difficulty in identifying all of them.

The Shakers made a variety of clocks: tall case, miniature, later called grandmother clocks, shelf, and wag-on-the-wall. As would be expected, the Shaker clocks were not as elegant as those made in the outside world; instead, they were very plain. Also, as would be expected, they were very well done. It would appear that the Shakers made clocks only in the North. I'm not sure whether or not they made any after the middle of the 1800s.

A tall case clock is a long-pendulum clock in a tall case. The cases stand from around 7 to 9½ feet tall. For most of these, the case was made in two pieces. The upper section is called a hood and covers the works and the clock face; the lower section is called the pendulum case, and consists of the waist and base. The grandmother clock has the same pieces and features; it just is shorter. The wag-on-the-wall, of course, is a pendulum clock without a case, designed to hang from the wall or sit on a special shelf.

As I have said over and over, you can't know too much when looking at antique furniture with buying in mind. This applies every bit as well to clocks, maybe more so in some respects. A good cabinetmaker can take a wag-on-the-wall and some old wood; and, with a bit of woodworking talent, turn them into a very convincing tall case clock. Fortunately, there aren't that many good woodworkers who have to resort to fakery to make a living; but, watch out for the obvious, as well as the not so obvious, especially if you are in the market for a clock.

Don't buy a tall case clock without looking it over; or, have an antiques dealer or cabinetmaker you trust check it for you. Watch for new-looking wood on the inside of the case. Question new or "replaced" feet; by changing the style of the feet, a clock can be made to appear to be of an earlier period. Look for good shrinkage in the

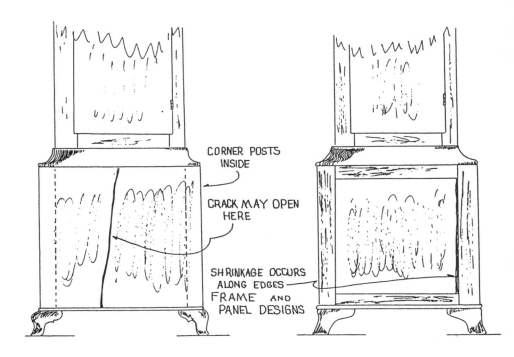

CORNER POSTS INSIDE

CRACK MAY OPEN HERE

SHRINKAGE OCCURS ALONG EDGES

FRAME AND PANEL DESIGNS

vertical backboard, and in the front of the base. The backboard of the waist and base should be one piece; often, because of the way these clocks were constructed, the front board will show shrinkage, either with a noticeable crack or with some shrinkage at the corners. When examining the backboard, be sure it is held in place with cut nails, all of the same style and age. Also, check the gap between the backboard, which should be set in a rabbeted out area, and the edge of the case for evidence of age. You should see old-looking wood and some dust, not new-looking, raw wood and modern tool marks.

Check the hood carefully; a lot of cases and hoods become separated for one reason or another through the years. Think about it for a minute. If a case has a new hood in one place, and a hood has a new case in another, it is conceivable to make two clocks from one by adapting a wag-on-the-wall to one of the "new" clocks. This would not be easy. But, at the current price for a tall case clock, it might be worth the effort for a good woodworker. I am not trying to imply that all clocks are reworked or that all cabinetmakers or antique furniture restorers are fakers; but, I see a lot of this going on, especially with items as expensive and rare as tall case clocks. Again, you cannot be too careful when looking at antique furniture.

Another reason to be sure the hood isn't a replacement is that a little reworking of a plane base and a fancier hood might turn a plane, medium-priced clock into an expensive "period" piece. Examine every joint and inside area you can. If the bottom of the base has been replaced or is broken, don't get too upset; this may have happened when a weight broke loose and fell. Believe me, when that happens, particularly if the weight is high in the case, the crashing noise is something you don't forget; and, indeed, it does break out the bottom of the case! I've had it happen!

Check the pillars in the hood; be sure they weren't "updated". On some clocks, the pillars may be a different wood, often a hardwood painted black or *ebonized.* If the clock has any *marquetry*, inlaid woods, usually of different colors to form a design of some sort, check the case and the hood; the marquetry design should carry over to, and be similar in, both. Also, be sure any marquetry wasn't a later addition to raise the value of the clock.

Some plain, softwood clocks were painted. They often had a lot of floral designs with lots of tendril vines painted on the hood door, as well as on the columns on either side of the case door. Some clocks were decorated with wax; the design was worked into the wood with cutting tools; then, it was filled with colored waxes; this was sort of between marquetry and paint, easier than marquetry, but harder to do than painting. These simple, plain clocks are well worth checking out very carefully. I have seen several rather new cases with old looking paint covering them, and, most likely, an old wag-on-the-wall inside.

When checking paint on one of these cases, look for evidence of paint in cracks where there should be only dust. Be sure the paint is worn where it should be, such as around the knobs on the doors and anyplace where some rubbing might occur from time to time. If the glass in the hood is supposedly original, it should be held in place with a very hard putty. Early putty is so hard it is nearly impossible to remove. So, if the putty is soft, find out why. Also, if the door in the hood has miter joints, be sure they have shrunk in the right places; if not, again, ask why.

If you find a tall case clock which you are in love with, can't live without, can afford, and, most of all, trust, but, it is too tall for your home, what do you do? You might be able to change the height

GAPS OCCUR DUE TO SHRINKAGE

TALL CASE CLOCK HOOD DOOR

enough by removing a finial, if it has one. If that isn't going to work, consider having a reliable woodworker, one who works on and understands antique furniture, remove the feet. ALWAYS KEEP THE FEET! By no means should you allow anyone to cut down the clock. Cut a hole in your ceiling first! I once cut a hole in a ceiling in order to get a corner cupboard into a house. I then applied a molding to hide the terrible hole left in the plaster; but, I didn't ruin the cupboard! If the clock won't fit by removing the finial or the feet, maybe you shouldn't buy it; or, if you must have it, store the clock until you have a home where it will fit.

Tall case clocks are an expensive investment in today's antique furniture market; so, be very careful when shopping for one. If you find a clock with a damaged case, you may be able to have the repairs done by a good cabinetmaker. If the case only needs regluing and some minor repairs, it would be all right to do the work yourself. However, if the case is really bad with lots of molding missing, or a door missing, or something of that sort, take it to a good restorer; it is worth preserving the value. As for the works, I can only recommend that you find a skilled clockmaker or restorer. Make certain that whoever he is he knows how to work on early clocks. I would try to get a recommendation from a couple of reliable antiques dealers or from a friend. Expect this to be expensive; but, if the clock is any good, restoring it will be worthwhile. I can't think of many sounds which are more soothing in the home than the slow ticking of a tall case clock.

WALL CUPBOARDS

Now, let's discuss a very abundant case piece: the *cupboard*. There are a great number of different types of cupboards; they were used both for storage and display, and a combination of the two. Cupboards are called by different names depending upon the period of time, their use, and the part of the country they came from, as well as their shape. For example, one which fits into a corner is called a corner cupboard, while one that sits flat against the wall is known as a wall cupboard.

First, I'll talk about wall cupboards, the flat-back type of cupboards which sits against a wall. The earliest ones you are likely to see are *court cupboards*. The best place to see one of these is in a museum. To find one in an antiques shop or show would be very unlikely. If you do see one for sale it probably is a Wallace Nutting reproduction, most of which are marked in some way. Another type of early cupboard which you're not likely to run into at the local antiques show is a *press cupboard*. The main difference between these two is that the court cupboard is open at the bottom while the press cupboard is not. When examining one of these cases, it is quite difficult to tell English-made ones from their American-made counterparts. The most significant difference is in the secondary woods.

The English usually used oak for drawer bottoms, etc. while the American cabinetmakers used pine most of the time. These case pieces date from the mid to late 17th century. While I am talking about the early types, a third, even rarer, is the *livery cupboard*. Most of these are either English or reproductions. These cupboards were open between wooden bars; and, most had locks. Apparently, they were used for food storage—the open area allowed air to circulate to keep the food from spoiling, while the lock and key kept the hungry servants from helping themselves when no one was watching.

The three types of cupboards mentioned here were only for the wealthy. Common folks didn't have the room for such pieces, had little or nothing to put into them, and didn't have the money to have them made.

Now, on to wall cupboards to which all of us can relate. Early 18th century examples started to become simpler in design; and, they didn't look as "English" as their predecessors. These wall cupboards also were built for the more affluent, and often were used to show off their belongings. An example of this is the *dresser*, which is referred

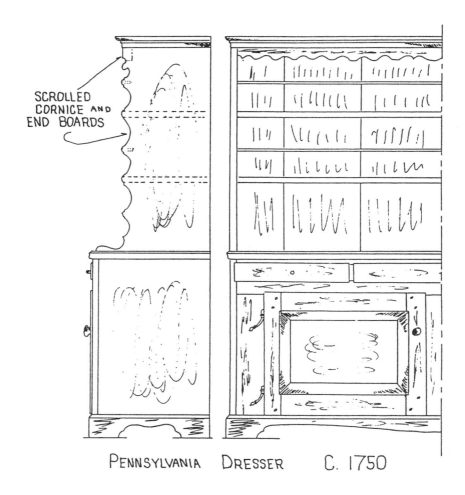

SCROLLED CORNICE ᴬᴺᴰ END BOARDS

PENNSYLVANIA DRESSER   C. 1750

to as a *pewter cupboard*. The name dresser apparently came from the French *dressoir* which was a cupboard with open shelves used to display china, pewter, etc. The earliest reference I could find to a dressoir was a photo of an example dating from the 15th century; and, it really looked more like a court cupboard. Anyway, whether you prefer the name pewter cupboard or the term dresser, it seems to be one and the same.

The biggest problem with buying a dresser is you always must check to be sure it wasn't once an ordinary cupboard which lost its doors along the way. Dressers are much scarcer and therefore more expensive than cupboards with doors, especially if the doors are

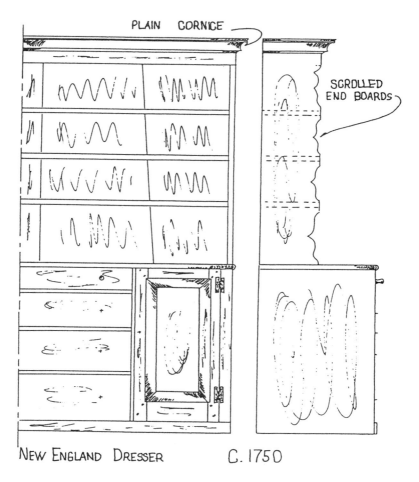

PLAIN CORNICE

SCROLLED END BOARDS

NEW ENGLAND DRESSER   C. 1750

damaged or missing altogether. Check for evidence of doors; look for old hinge marks. Check for rub marks on the top surface of the counter where door bottoms may have rubbed. Since dressers usually do not have stiles, look to be sure there are no nail holes where stiles may have been. Also, check the front edges of the end boards; be sure there are no new saw marks which would indicate the scrolling was newly cut.

Generally, New England dressers can be told from their Pennsylvania counterparts by two things other than wood. First, most New England dressers do not have spoon racks; and second, the lower part of the cornice usually is straight. The Pennsylvania examples, on the other hand, often have spoon racks, generally cut into the front

UPPER DOORS AND STILE REMOVED ∿ END STILES CUT BACK

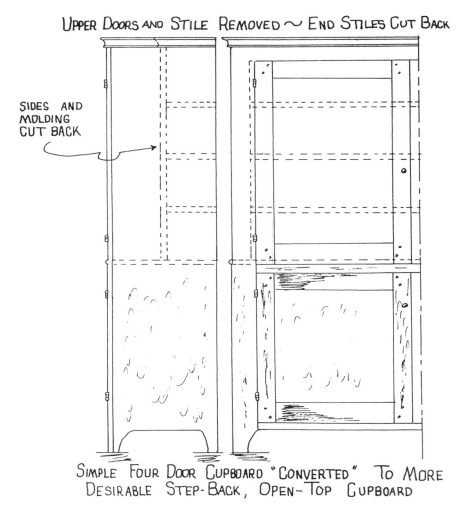

SIDES AND
MOLDING
CUT BACK

SIMPLE FOUR DOOR CUPBOARD "CONVERTED" TO MORE
DESIRABLE STEP-BACK, OPEN-TOP CUPBOARD

edge of the bottom shelf; and, the lower edge of the cornice usually is cut out similarly to the front edge of the sides with scrolling or scalloping. Dressers, like many other pieces of early furniture, were made in many countries such as Canada, England, France, and America. And, except for the woods used, it sometimes is rather difficult to tell just where a piece originated. The best thing to do is visit museums and house restorations to see the pieces displayed, how they look, and what types of woods were used. Most of these cupboards from America seem to have been made during the 18th century. By the 19th century, the majority of the cupboards this size had doors on them.

Many wall cupboards often are called *hutches;* I never had been sure where that term came from; so, I did a bit of research. The best I can come up with is a definition from one of my old reference books which says the word *hutch* comes from the French *huche,* which is a cabinet or chest with doors, usually on legs. Sounds a bit like an early court cupboard! My old dictionary defines a hutch as "a chest, box, coffer, bin, coop or the like; as, a grain hutch; a rabbit hutch. To put away; hoard." So, I guess you could call a cupboard, cabinet, or anything else where you store or "hoard" things, a hutch. I always have had difficulty calling anything other than a rabbit coop a hutch; probably my farm background! However, hutch technically is correct.

Through the 18th century and into the early 19th century, wall cupboards were made in nearly any combination of drawers, doors, and open areas that the cabinetmaker/designer could think of or was capable of building. We see small, hanging cupboards, large one and two-piece units, small one and two-piece units, cupboards over cupboards and cupboards over drawers. Some had solid panel doors or were *blind*, while others had doors that were glazed, with *lights* or panes of glass. In bedrooms, there appeared *wardrobes*, some with drawers, some with shelves, and many with both. Some wardrobes were plain and practical; others were elaborate such as *kases*. There are flat-front cupboards with one or two long, full-length doors hiding many shelves. And, there are step-back cupboards with doors in the upper section, doors in the lower section, and one, two, or three drawers in between. Some step-back cupboards have a *pie shelf* between the upper and lower sections, either one-piece or two-piece units. These open pie shelves seem to be mostly on eastern and central Pennsylvania cupboards, leading to the local name of *Dutch cupboard*.

Wall cupboard designs varied with the area and the wealth of the people for whom they were being made. Most of these cupboards, whether built-in or free standing, were custom made by local cabinetmakers. Of course, the ability and talent of the cabinetmaker had a great deal to do with the elaborateness of the unit. Among the very plain cupboards, you have Shaker pieces, usually closed, and often with a combination of doors and drawers. The attention paid to detail is your best way of identifying a Shaker piece. Again, visit Shaker museums and collections to get a first-hand view of Shaker cupboards. Unfortunately, some of the later Shaker pieces aren't as well made as those of the outside world. If you're looking for a Shaker piece, expect to pay more than you would for a non-Shaker cupboard; and, because of that, be sure you are getting a Shaker-built unit. Just because someone says it is Shaker doesn't make it so; check every detail. Ask where it originated, what community, and compare it to other cupboards made by the Shakers in that community. The safest way to be sure is to have the piece checked by an expert.

Until the late 1800s when built-in closets appeared in many new homes, nearly every room could use a wall cupboard of some sort. They were found in the kitchen and pantry as storage and work units; they were used in the dining or eating area for storage, and in the bedroom as a press and/or wardrobe. The bedroom units ranged from the very simple, plain wardrobe to the elaborate, finely designed press. As people became more affluent, and acquired more "trappings", they needed places to store, hoard, or show off these acquisitions. Of course, this started in the cities where much of the wealth was. As the money filtered out to the rural areas, more and more country people needed cupboards of some sort in which to keep their new belongings, whether china, pewter, or clothing. Except for Shaker cupboards, the plainer the case piece, the simpler the cabinetmaker and the final owner. The most elaborate wall cupboards were made in the Philadelphia, Boston, or New York areas by well-trained cabinetmakers, often people who trained abroad or apprenticed under foreign-born cabinetmakers here in America.

Many of these early wall cupboards, whether of soft or hardwood, were painted. Some were painted very plainly; others were quite fancy. In the early to mid 1800s, some were painted to look like a different wood than that from which they were made. I have seen a lot of painted cupboards, some very well done, some terrible, and lots repainted; but, the one I'll never forget was the really nice walnut dresser which originally had been painted blue. In the mid to late 1800s, it was repainted to look like oak. I could never quite understand why anyone would want a nice worn blue walnut cupboard to look like oak. I realize it was the vogue of the day.

When checking for repainted pieces, always look for patches under "original paint"; obviously, there shouldn't be any! Check for brush marks; sometimes, when a unit is repainted, someone will apply the paint very sparingly, to give the impression that it has been worn off through the years. If that is the case, you wouldn't see brush marks! Look for chipped or worn paint areas under the last coat; there shouldn't be any. Examine for another color under the present paint;

there may be a red wash, which appears more like a stain than paint. But, there shouldn't be another color of paint, if the coat you are looking at is truly original. Examine the back and under the skirt, if there is one, for evidence of another color. Also, check drawer sides, again, if there are drawers.

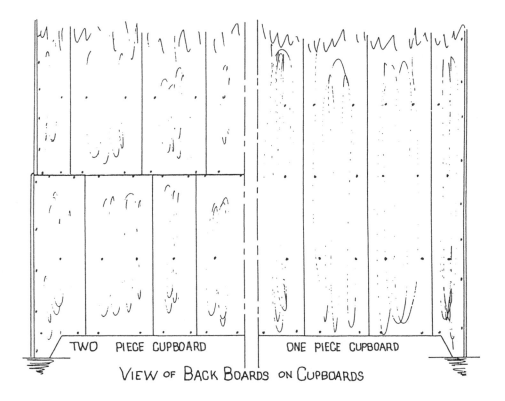

TWO PIECE CUPBOARD   ONE PIECE CUPBOARD

VIEW OF BACK BOARDS ON CUPBOARDS

If the wall cupboard is a two-piece unit, be sure both pieces started out together. Examine the construction in both the top and bottom sections. All of the joints, and so on, should be made the same; also, the woods and color of the wood in both units should match. Another thing about a large, two-piece cupboard you should check out—was it ever a one-piece unit? Look at the back; and examine the backboards for this information. If the boards in both the top and bottom are the same width and match up vertically, the cupboard most likely was cut in half. This may have made it easier to handle, or move; but, it also devalues the piece a bit.

Two Types of Jam Cupboards
C. 1840 -1860

Another type of wall cupboard which has become very popular, mostly because of its smaller size, is the *jam cupboard*. Almost any small cupboard seems to get this name tagged onto it. Generally, jam or jelly cupboards are short, about 5 to 6 feet high or less, with one or two drawers at the top, and one or two doors in the bottom area. Some jam cupboards have flat, plain tops, while others have galleries. The later in the Victorian period they were made, the more elaborate the galleries. This same type of cupboard, usually built a few years later and with pierced tin panels in place of the wood ones in the doors and sometimes also in the sides, is called a *safe*. Most jam cupboards seem to have been made between 1840 and 1880, while few pie safes are that early. The majority of them seem to date from 1870 to around 1910. Also, a lot of pie safes are from the South, many from the Virginia area.

While I'm on the subject of storage units, I shouldn't overlook the shelves which often were made throughout the same period we're talking about here. I realize they are not case pieces; but, they did take the place of cupboards when people couldn't afford the real thing. Some stood freely; many, however, were built in. And, some could be called case pieces. They had a back and doors on the bottom

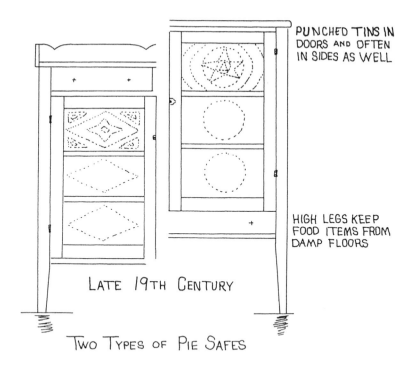

PUNCHED TINS IN DOORS AND OFTEN IN SIDES AS WELL

HIGH LEGS KEEP FOOD ITEMS FROM DAMP FLOORS

LATE 19TH CENTURY

TWO TYPES OF PIE SAFES

section. I have heard these called *bucket benches, milk benches,* and *shelves.* These open units are among the easiest to reproduce or fake; so, if you are in the market for such an item, do be careful. Check everything I have written about regarding nails, paint, patina, and construction.

CORNER CUPBOARDS

Corner Cupboards are one of the few pieces of furniture which haven't changed much through the years. Except for ornamentation, it is hard to put a date on a lot of these popular pieces. Generally speaking, most corner cupboards were made from about 1725 to the first quarter of the 1800s; I'm not sure why, but with the coming of the Empire period, people didn't have as many corner cupboards made. However, built-in cupboards continued, although not as numerous, for another century.

Corner cupboards probably are one of the most practical pieces of furniture ever designed and made. Nearly every home could use them; and, they fit into almost any room. The ones made for the kitchen or pantry area usually were pine or poplar and often were either painted or unfinished. A corner cupboard to be used in the dining or some other room often was made of mahogany, walnut, cherry, or another good-looking wood. A large number of these cupboards were painted, even the hardwood pieces. Many corner cupboards had glazed doors on the top and panel doors on the bottom; a good number were open at the top and panelled at the bottom; and, some had panel doors in both the top and bottom sections.

These cupboards can be found in styles ranging from very simple to quite elaborate. As with most pieces of furniture, the fancier the piece, the more important the owner, or at least he had the money required to have such a cupboard made, while a plainer, simpler piece tends to have been made for a less wealthy family. However, even the more affluent had simple corner cupboards in their kitchens. Corner cupboard styles more or less follow the styles of the wall cupboard as far as area of manufacture. This applies to the types of wood used, the design of moldings, and, in some cases, the kind of feet.

As for hardware, many cupboards made before 1800 had H or HL hinges. The pine or poplar cupboards usually had wrought iron hinges which were painted the same as the cupboard, if it was painted; in contrast, many of the nice hardwood cupboards had brass hinges. The plain cupboards usually had wooden pulls and turn knobs, while their more elegant counterparts had brass knobs and pulls. Most of the closed-top cupboards had locks on the doors; often, when locks were used, there were no pulls of any type. The door would be opened by turning and then pulling on the key.

When looking for a corner cupboard today, you should try to get the right style for the area in which you are going to use it. For example, if you want one for a corner in your kitchen or your country diningroom, by all means, find a simple, plain cupboard. If your diningroom is more formal or you plan to use the cupboard in your livingroom to show off some of your collection, look for a more formal piece. If you search long enough, you should be able to find the right style. There are nice hardwood corner cupboards which are quite plain, if your decorations are simple; and, of course, you can find hardwood cupboards which are quite elegant, with plain, fluted, or carved pilasters, dentil molding, heavy cornice, shell-tops, curved backs, and other fine details.

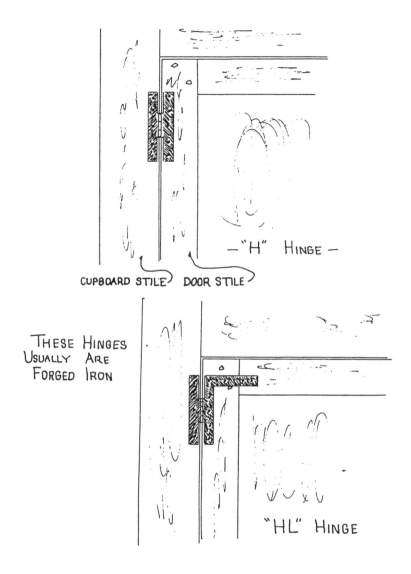

— "H" Hinge —

CUPBOARD STILE   DOOR STILE

These Hinges
Usually Are
Forged Iron

"HL" Hinge

Some of the open top, plain cupboards are very similar to the dressers of the same period and same area. Many corner cupboards, both fancy and plain, have *butterfly* cut-out shelves. These nicely curved shelves usually are found on open-top cupboards; but, they also were used on closed-top cupboards, both with glazed and panelled doors. If the cupboard was made in Pennsylvania, there is a good chance you will find that it has spoon cut-outs, like a dresser

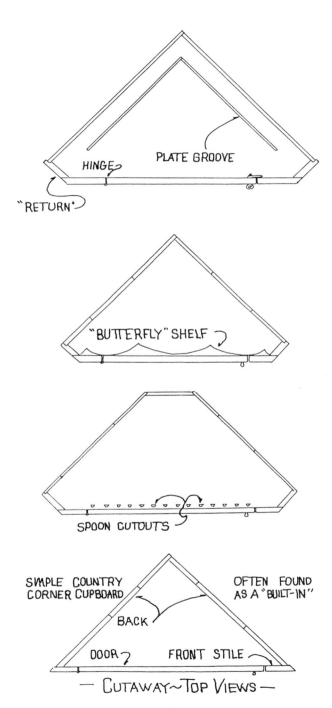

PLATE GROOVE

HINGE

"RETURN"

"BUTTERFLY" SHELF

SPOON CUTOUTS

SIMPLE COUNTRY
CORNER CUPBOARD

OFTEN FOUND
AS A "BUILT-IN"

BACK

DOOR   FRONT STILE

— CUTAWAY~TOP VIEWS —

from the same area. I have seen these cut-outs on butterfly shelves; usually, however, they are on straight shelves.

A nice touch to watch for on a glazed door cupboard is the lining up of the shelves and the door mullions. If they are not lined up, it generally means the cabinetmaker lacked the aesthetic values required to do such things.

Since a corner cupboard was made for one specific area or spot, it didn't get moved around a lot from room to room. Because of this, it didn't suffer the damage a lot of other cupboards did. Most corner cupboards are in pretty good shape as compared to their flat counterparts. The main damage to corner cupboards seems to be rotted bases or feet, most often found on plain pine or poplar pieces, since they often were used on dirt or damp floors. The finer cupboards rarely have any damage to their bases.

The other thing which sometimes happened to both plain and fancy corner cupboards was damage to their doors. The glazed doors often are quite heavy due to all of the glass; and, sometimes, the frames were too light for the weight. This caused the doors either to sag or come apart, many times both. When this happened, the doors usually were removed and often lost.

So, if you are looking at an open-top cupboard, be sure it isn't one of these. Always check for evidence of doors by examining the stiles of the case for hinge cut-outs or for where a knob or lock may have been. If it is a simple cupboard with an open top, check to be sure the hinge cut-outs weren't removed by making the opening a bit larger. A good place to look is in the upper corners of the open area. Check where the stiles and the top cross-pieces join.

Another type of corner cupboard, which isn't too popular, is the built-in unit. Many of these are very elegant with lots of architectural details. A few were quite plain, especially the ones built into kitchens or simple diningrooms. But, many were pretty elaborate. All of these cupboards were not built into corners; some were built into the side wall of a room and often had rounded or curved backs. They usually were made of pine. Most often, they were painted the color of the woodwork in the room. The moldings and details were the same as the surrounding room. It is difficult to remove one of these cupboards and use it elsewhere, unless it is removed very carefully, and then built into its new home. Once in a while, I see a cupboard which was a built-in used as a regular, free-standing corner cupboard; it works, but usually looks exactly like what it is. Some built-ins are only a front with shelves; and, they can't be removed and used elsewhere without adding a back and doing some other woodwork. I feel that if you are going to buy a built-in corner cupboard, it should be built into the corner, or wall, the same way as it originally was. It is very rare that built-ins can be used successfully any other way.

There was a revival of corner cupboards in the early 1900s, mostly full-sized, but also some smaller hanging ones. Covered with a lot of paint, one of these could turn up at an auction. And, not looking too closely, you might end up owning it, if you are not careful. These pieces were not made as fakes; but, with fifty to seventy years of use and a lot of paint, someone may try to pass one off. They often were made either of oak or yellow pine, and usually rather narrow boards. The backs of these pieces almost always are made from very narrow boards or plywood. The nails are 20th century; and, the wood, especially the backboards, shows power tool marks. They are not that hard to spot, if you know they exist, and if you have some idea of what to look for.

A couple of more tips when looking at corner cupboards—a lot of them were made in one piece. For one reason or another, many later were cut in half. This makes the cupboard a lot easier to handle; but, it also devalues it. If you are looking at a two-piece unit, check the backboards carefully to see if it has been cut or if it always was a two-piece cupboard. If it always was a two-piece unit, the backboards should not line up, top and bottom.

HANGING CUPBOARDS

Still another case piece which is rather popular is the *hanging cupboard*, both wall and corner. There were some small cupboards made to hang or set on a table or counter; but, many of the hanging wall cupboards I see started out as the tops of something else. For example, there are a lot of early to mid-Victorian desk tops being called "hanging cupboards". If you look closely at the bottom edge, both front and sides, you often will see a shadow where the piece sat into a frame or molding on a small desk. Also, when looking at one of these cupboards, check the back to see if it ever was hung. How was it fastened to the wall? The bottom board of the cupboard should show some signs of finish, not as much as the front and sides, but as much as the top. If it was the top of a desk, the bottom will show no color or finish; instead, it may be rather rough. Hanging cupboards are great, quite useful, and take up little room. So, therefore, they

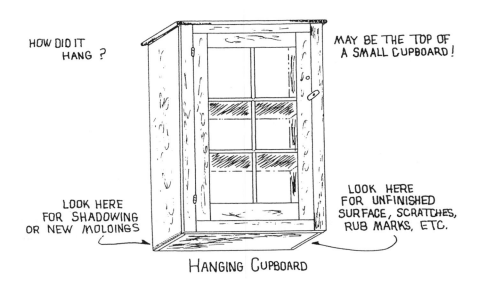

HOW DID IT
HANG ?

MAY BE THE TOP OF
A SMALL CUPBOARD!

LOOK HERE
FOR SHADOWING
OR NEW MOLOINGS

LOOK HERE
FOR UNFINISHED
SURFACE, SCRATCHES,
RUB MARKS, ETC.

HANGING CUPBOARD

often are faked; be careful when looking for one. Check all of the joints to be sure the piece wasn't a larger cupboard which at one time was damaged and has been cut down to become a more desirable item.

Generally, the early hanging cupboards had panel doors, while the later ones had glazed doors. All of this coincided with the larger cupboards of the same period. However, panel doors do not make a cupboard 18th century; the later Victorian desk tops I mentioned often had panelled doors. If you know anything about antique furniture periods, you certainly should be able to tell an 18th century door from a later Victorian one. The later panel doors usually have thinner panels, while the earlier ones often have raised panels; this is the easiest way to tell, if you are not sure. Of course, if you are not sure, or have questions which can't be answered, maybe you should leave the piece where it is!

Some of the early hanging cupboards had outside shelves, either on the top or under the case. You aren't likely to see this feature on later units, and not too often on the early ones. Most hanging cupboards have one or two inside shelves, depending upon the size of the case.

Hanging cupboards were made of the same woods as their larger counterparts, and in similar styles. Both the hard and softwood pieces often were painted. Once in a while, you may see a nice, early, hanging cupboard, usually of walnut and from Pennsylvania, with spoon cut-outs either inside or along the front edge of a shelf under the main case. These are rare and usually rather expensive, if you can find one. Also, because of their scarcity, they are faked. Be careful!

Your best buy for a simple, plain, pine or poplar, hanging cupboard may be the top of a desk. I'm not suggesting that everyone run out and turn desk tops into small hanging cupboards; but, if you see one for sale, and it is reasonably priced, it does make a nice hanging unit.

Another type of hanging cupboard is the hanging corner cupboard. There aren't as many of these as wall cupboards, partly because they aren't as easy to fake by using something else and then calling it a hanging corner cupboard. Most of the hanging corner cupboards you see are either authentic or reproductions, but rarely faked from something else. Look for new-looking joints, wrong types of nails, modern tool marks, etc. when checking for a reproduction.

Another thing to always watch for is this: when a piece, especially something like a hanging corner cupboard, looks exactly like one in a well-known reference book, be suspicious. Early pieces were made one at a time; and, even though a certain woodworker may have made several such units, and one shows up in a reference book, the chances of finding an exact copy are pretty slim, unless, of course, it was made from the photo in that book! Again, be careful. The periods of hanging corner cupboards are about the same as full-size corner cupboards; and, like the full-size units, the hardware and woods are about the same.

Something to watch for in both hanging and full-size corner cupboards is *inlay*. It doesn't show up much, but occasionally is found, and usually was done during the Hepplewhite period (1790–1810), often in a walnut case made either in Pennsylvania or Virginia. This inlay generally is authentic; but, it pays to check carefully to be sure, as carefully as you would check any other part of a piece of antique furniture.

DRY SINKS

Dry sinks have come a long way since they first were used for cleaning and washing things. They now can be found pictured on the covers of glossy magazines and in some rather fancy antiques shops and

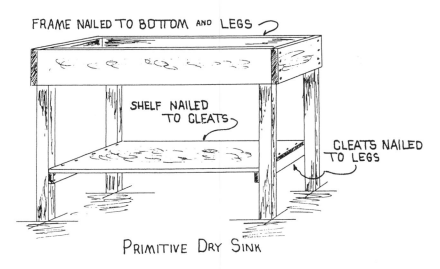

FRAME NAILED TO BOTTOM AND LEGS

SHELF NAILED
TO CLEATS

CLEATS NAILED
TO LEGS

PRIMITIVE DRY SINK

elegant shows. I wasn't able to find out much about the earliest dry sinks; most of the ones I have seen or read about date from around 1800 at the earliest. The ones from this period were rather primitive and not made to last very long. As these sinks rotted or became loose due to heavy use, they were broken up, the scrap wood used in the fireplace, and a new sink built. Each time a new one was made, it was mostly likely advanced a little in style and design. Many of the earliest ones were made of old or scrap wood which might have been on hand. Around 1810 to 1830, more elaborate dry sinks started to appear; they more or less resembled the other case pieces being made at that time. The basins of these later dry sinks usually were lined with zinc or tin and often had drain holes. In many cases, the hole had a lead pipe in it to drain away the water from the sink into a bucket or through the wall to outdoors.

Some dry sinks have a drawer, while others have an upper section with three or four drawers; and, still others have a cupboard built above, with doors and drawers. Dry sinks were made all over early America, north, south, east, and west. Most of the ones we find for sale today are from the East Coast, including New England, and inland to western New York and Ohio. When folks moved westward, they took a lot of their furnishings; but, the dry sink was not one of the items they moved. It often was broken up for firewood, or just left behind to rot away. Because of the way they were used and built, early dry sinks didn't have a long life span.

EASY TO FAKE— BE SURE THIS STYLE DRY SINK
WASN'T SOME OTHER PIECE OF FURNITURE AT ANOTHER
TIME!

DRY SINK C. 1870-1880

The demand for dry sinks has far surpassed the availability of good, honest, early ones. Therefore, a lot of reproductions or fakes have been made. I remember a woodworker in eastern Pennsylvania, thirty to thirty-five years ago, making dry sinks using pine boards from old barns and other buildings being torn down in the area. These sinks were made as reproductions at the time. However, since they were put together using dovetails and cut nails, also taken from the old buildings, and were made very similarly to the ones from the early 1800s, today it would be difficult for the average person to distinguish one of these sinks from a truly old one without having the two sitting next to each other. With the current interest in country furnishings, the demand for sinks is stronger than ever. And, as in the past, there are a lot of talented woodworkers willing to supply that demand!

When looking at a dry sink, be sure it wasn't once a small cupboard which has had a sink added to the top. Check the top boards very carefully to be sure they are as old as the lower section; and, look for evidence of lots of wear and probably a little rot due to water. Because most people prefer a dry sink with a drawer, be sure the drawer is original. It isn't too difficult to add a drawer to a sink which never had one. If the sink you are looking at has a drawer, pull it out and check for evidence of the same color, if there is any, on the front edge of the side of the drawer and the inside edge of the frame which

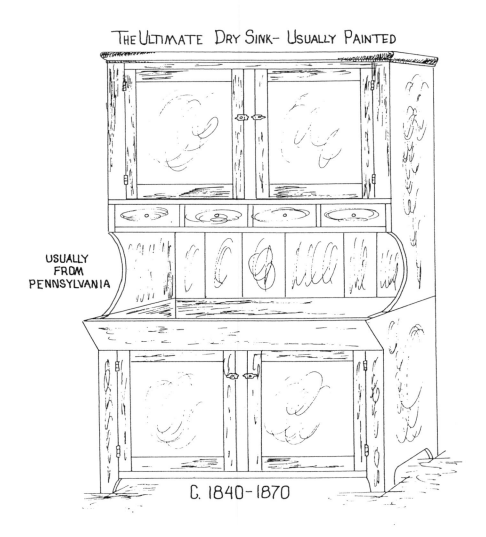

The Ultimate Dry Sink— Usually Painted

USUALLY
FROM
PENNSYLVANIA

C. 1840-1870

supports the drawer. While it is out, check inside the drawer opening. Does it look "right" in there? Check for machine marks where a
piece of wood may have been cut. Look for the wrong colors of finish
or raw wood edges. Watch for anything which may indicate that the
dry sink was altered to take a small drawer from some other piece of
furniture.

If you are looking at a nice, two-piece, dry sink with a cupboard
top, be sure the top is original to the base. Check everything I have

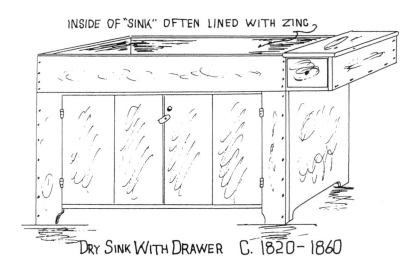

INSIDE OF "SINK" OFTEN LINED WITH ZINC

DRY SINK WITH DRAWER   C. 1820-1860

written about—types of nails and construction should match, up and down, as should woods, colors, and so on. This type of sink is-not very common, and often was from Pennsylvania.

Faking dry sinks is not new; and, as long as there is a demand, it will continue. I once saw a pine cottage commode, turned upside down, with its top removed, and some work done on the bottom so that it looked like a dry sink. Of course, the obvious give-away was that the doors were upside down; and, the top of the shelf inside had no wear while the bottom of that shelf had several marks on it which indicated that something was upside down. Since the shelf was set into a dado on each side, the commode itself must have been upside down! Close examination showed what had been done. Always look at every detail very carefully!

WOOD BOXES

Still another case piece is the *wood box*. These usually are rather low, around 20 inches high. Most of them are long, like an elongated blanket box, and in two sections, one smaller than the other. The smaller section was for keeping kindling while larger pieces of wood were stored in the other section. These boxes seem to be mostly 19th century; however, as with most country pieces, it is very hard to date

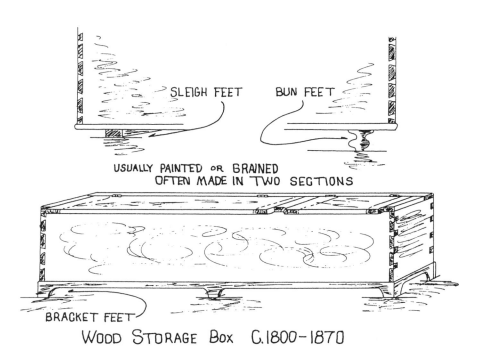

SLEIGH FEET   BUN FEET

USUALLY PAINTED or GRAINED
OFTEN MADE IN TWO SECTIONS

BRACKET FEET

WOOD STORAGE BOX   C.1800-1870

a wood box. You can find them with sleigh feet, bun feet, bracket feet, and with no feet. Some of the longer wood boxes have a center or fifth bun foot, a third sleigh foot, or center bracket foot; these extra feet were to support the weight from the wood which could be put in a longer box.

These boxes are quite useful in the home and are nicer pieces of furniture than grain bins. Wood boxes usually are dovetailed and often are found in paint, some with grain painting. They make good toy boxes, if you have the space in your child's room for one. Also a wood box would make a comfortable window seat if you have the spot for it. They are great for storage of almost anything, including wood for your wood stove or fireplace!

I haven't seen any faked wood boxes that I knew of; but, I do see them with faked paint once in a while. They seem to be a favorite box for people to grain paint; that isn't to say that all of the grain-painted wood boxes you see are faked. But, do watch for repainted ones. The new paint may be covering some repairs which you should know about. Again, be careful.

Sugar Chests and Cellarets

Two other case pieces which aren't too popular in the northeastern United States are *sugar chests* or *safes* and *cellarets*. Sugar, like salt, spices, and tea, was very hard to come by and expensive. Because of this, it was kept under lock and key. Sugar was purchased in cones wrapped in blue paper. These cones were stored; when sugar was needed, someone with a key opened the sugar chest and, with a pair of sugar nippers or cutters, nipped off a piece of sugar. Then, the safe was locked again.

The other case piece, the cellaret, was a storage bin for wine and other spirits. They can be found in the north; but, most are from the south. They were made over a long period of time which is evident by the succession of styles that can be found, which range from Queen Anne to Sheraton.

Although most sugar chests and cellarets are of rather high style, they certainly would fit into the country home, to be used as a small bar or for some other type of storage. Most of them were made of cherry, walnut, or maple, and some of poplar. I'm sure they also can be found in mahogany; and, if you looked long enough, you might find a sugar chest in pine.

Grain Bins

Another case piece, which is as primitive as the early dry sink, is the *grain* or *feed bin*. These boxes also have become very popular in the past few years. They usually were made of pine or poplar, nailed together, and often with a slanted top which was easier to reach into. Many were painted. However, unlike dry sinks, these boxes were not found in every home. They were used on farms, large or small, to store grain for the cattle, horses, sheep, pigs, chickens, or whatever.

These bins are very useful in a country-decorated home as a catch-all, to store records, books, or your antiques publications. They work well in a "mud" room for children's boots or garden clothes; and, they are great places to put bags of dog or cat food so that your pets can't get into it in the middle of the night. If you are thinking of using a grain bin in your home as a piece of furniture, try to locate one with a flat area at the back. You will find that such a bin is much more useful than one where the lid hinges all the way in the rear, leaving no flat area on the top.

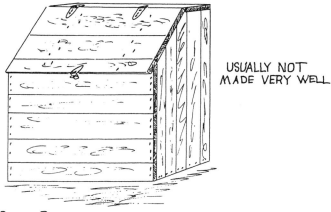

USUALLY NOT
MADE VERY WELL

GRAIN BIN— COULD BE ANY AGE— IDENTIFY BY
TOOL MARKS, NAILS, ETC.

Grain bins usually are rather dirty and often have rodent holes in them; the dirt is easy to clean. The rodent holes give the bins personality. They are not very expensive, and aren't often faked. Grain bins are nearly impossible to date; at best, you can only guess, maybe by the age of the barn it is in, the period of the nails in it, or perhaps by the tool marks in the wood; however, keep in mind, the nails and wood may be old; but, the box may have been made 20 years ago, and, since then, gotten beaten up pretty well in the barn. And, maybe a couple of rats have gnawed their way into it; by now, it may look 150 years old. If you are looking at one which you like, and you feel it is priced right for your purse, buy it. Don't worry too much about the age, that is unless it is quite obviously new.

TABLES

Basically, tables come in four different categories: trestle, sawbuck or "X" base, pedestal, and legged. These can be found in many types including dining tables, work tables, side tables, game tables, chair tables, bench tables, hutch tables, and on, and on!

TRESTLE TABLES

Originally, a *table* was only a loose board(s) resting on legs, probably resembling a trestle base, or on horses, similar to saw-horses, but a bit higher. After each meal, the table was taken apart and stored out of the way until it was needed again. Sometime during the Middle Ages, the fixed-base table appeared. However, the removable-top-table style has survived through the years and has been made in many periods. This style still is much sought after by many collectors of antique furniture. The loose top table available today is the frame base with attached legs, the frame often having a drawer or two. More about this style later.

A good, honest, early (before 1800), *trestle table* is almost impossible to find outside of a museum or private collection. The earliest, from the 17th century, a loose board sitting on two or three trestles, are extremely rare and most likely can be found only in museums. Later ones are almost as scarce. The construction of these tables made them rather vulnerable to becoming firewood! Wedges were lost, the feet became loose or even fell off the center post if the table had a three-piece trestle foot, stretchers were broken or lost, tops warped, cracked, or rotted, or all three, and tops became quite damaged from cutting and other daily wear. So, when the legged tables with skirts and, in many cases, base stretchers appeared, people couldn't wait to rid themselves of their trestle tables.

Even with all of the inherent problems, trestle tables are much sought after; and, because they are very scarce, they are faked a lot. I once examined a "great trestle table" for a customer. If the table had been right, it would have been a real bargain. If not, it was

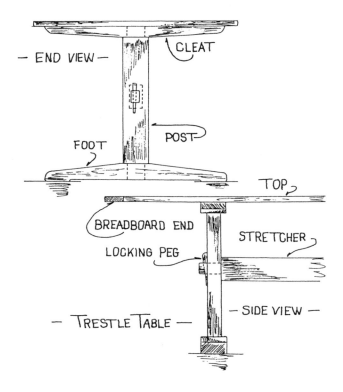

overpriced. What I found made it an over-priced fake. The base had been part of a quilting frame which had been cut down. Then, a one-piece board was nailed to it.

This board was seven feet long, twenty-three inches wide, and just about one inch thick, with no nail holes in the wrong places. The top of the board was scrubbed and had a great look. However, the underside was quite rough for a table top, showing some rough pit saw marks and a bit of hand-planing around the perimeter. Generally, table tops are planed smooth on the bottom, not always as cleanly as the top surface; but, they rarely show a lot of saw marks.

The base of this table was a typical trestle base, except that the wood was less than an inch thick. Even the feet and top supports were thin, very unusual for a base that had to support a top of this size. Close examination showed that the feet and supports had been cut down to fit the top width, and then stained. It was a fairly good job. However, the texture of the cut area felt different from the uncut area; and, the sheen of the cut area was different from the uncut.

With a bright light, I could see between the top support and the top. This showed me that there was no dirt or dust in the cracks; and, when the nails had come through the top, the wood broke away leaving some very raw-looking splinters in there. The stretcher showed almost no wear. Again, with a bright light, I could see raw wood where the stretcher end was cut to fit into the trestle, but only on one end; this indicated that the stretcher had been shortened to fit the top.

With this table, the top most likely was from a wall of an early house, with enough wood cut off of each end to get rid of any nail holes but still long enough to make a nice, one-board top. I pointed all of this out to the owners, who really didn't want to hear it. They loved the table. To this day, I do not know whether they returned or kept it. And, since they have moved, I may never know.

There still are a few trestle tables to be found at auctions, sales, and once in a while, at antiques shows and shops. They often are in rather rough condition or are fairly late, sometimes both. Because of their scarceness and popularity, be careful! They are easy to fake and well worth the effort in most cases. If you find one with a loose top, be very careful. If you find one with a "fixed top", usually nailed to the supports, check all of the areas I have mentioned. Another thing to examine is the nails; be sure all of them are the same size, from the same period, and that the heads are going in the right direction. The longest part of the head of a cut nail should run with the grain of the wood. Also, watch for marks around the nails made by a hammer head, called *half moons*. If there are any, question at least the originality of the top. Such marks shouldn't be there if the top was put on by an early cabinetmaker.

If the top is pegged, make certain the pegs are hand-shaved, not perfectly round dowels. Also, the heads of the pegs should protrude slightly above the surface of the top due to wear and shrinkage. As with any other piece of antique furniture, the color of the wood should be the same, have the right shading, etc.

If the table is painted, check to be sure all of the paint was put on at the same time. Painted or unpainted, all of the parts should look as though they started out together. If the stretcher has wedges, they may have been replaced. This is more or less allowable since they were so easily lost or broken. Because most fixed top trestle tables have the stretchers pegged to the trestle, there may not be many wedges to worry about. I have not seen many trestle tables

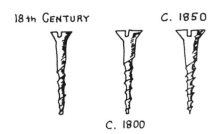

18th CENTURY   C. 1850

C. 1800

on the market that I trusted. So, if you are looking for one, do be careful.

Dating a trestle table is very difficult. About all that you have to go by is the way the wood was worked, nails, and, occasionally, screws. As I have pointed out, early trestle tables are not likely to be found on the market. With this information, if you are looking for one, you know that if it is supposed to be 17th or early 18th century, it quite possibly is a fake, or reproduction.

If the top is nailed down with really nice rose-head nails, be very suspicious; generally, these nails were not used in such places. Also, does the rest of the table look like it has been used since the early to mid 1700s? If the top is fastened by screws going through the supports, into the underside of the table, remove a screw and look at the end. If it is pointed, it was made after 1846. That's when the pointed screw was patented. If it is flat on the end, and the screw driver slot is a bit off center, then, most likely, the screw is from before that time. If a flat end screw looks like it may be machine-made, then it could be early 19th century. Up until the late 18th century, screws were hand made, one by one. That is one reason you don't see a lot of them in early pieces of furniture.

The Shakers made a lot of trestle tables, some quite long. Their tables usually had a different foot than other tables, and the bases more often were made of a hard wood such as walnut, cherry, or maple than were table bases made outside of the Shaker communities. Also, the tops were made of hardwood from time to time, something rarely done be non-Shaker furniture makers.

Think of where a trestle table was used, how it was used, how often it was used, and how dirty early homes were, often with dirt floors; then, take a good look at the table for sale. Try to understand how much use and abuse it should show. Now, try to date it; a table used for 200 to 250 years under these conditions would show a lot of wear. Again, as always with antique furniture, you can't know too much.

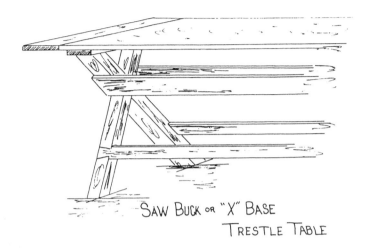

SAW BUCK or "X" BASE
TRESTLE TABLE

SAWBUCK TABLES

These tables date back nearly as far as trestle tables. Also called trestle tables by some, they are sometimes referred to as *X base* tables or *braced base* tables. Again, the earliest had loose tops and were taken apart after each meal to be put out of the way so that the family had room in which to move around. Remember, most early settler families were rather large; and, their first homes were quite small. So, being able to get the *board* out of the way was advantageous. After a certain period, the *sawbuck* tops, bases, and stretchers were fastened together; this is the type of sawbuck most often found today. They are a lot more plentiful than trestle tables, usually with a fixed top which was not big, often only three feet long. Most sawbucks started life in New England; but, examples can be found from other areas. Checking the wood is the best way to get some idea of where a table is from. Many also have a nice red, blue, or yellow paint on them. If you see a painted sawbuck table, examine the paint carefully.

All of the things to look for when checking a trestle table also apply to the sawbuck. The main difference between these two styles, other than design, is that there are a lot more sawbuck tables on the

market that are right than trestle tables. You still must look at every
thing very carefully because there are fakes out there; however, I
don't feel these tables are faked as much as others. Just to be sure,
check nails, wood age, wear and tear on the feet and stretchers, and
everything else you can think of. If you see a sawbuck which is a bit
loose, be careful. A lot of the smaller ones were degraded to the
porch or a shed and may be suffering from dry rot or worms. If that
is the case, they usually are very hard to tighten up. In fact, if it is
bad enough, you may need to have several new pieces made in order
to make the table useful. If it needs a lot replaced, you may be better
off having one built. So, if you see a sawbuck which is a "little loose",
be sure it is easily repairable before you buy it.

Small sawbuck tables are useful as occasional tables or serving
pieces. But, many of them are very hard to sit at for dining. If that is
your reason for getting one, be sure to try it with your type of chair
before you buy.

I have seen some late, 1850 to 1870, sawbuck tables which have
loose tops; they come apart just like the 17th and early 18th century
pieces. Such tables seem to have been made for and used by
churches, or something of that sort. They are easy to tell from their
earlier cousins. The tops are hardly an inch thick; and, the bases are
made of rather lightweight wood. In each case, the table never was
painted, and shows a lot of wear and weathering. They look good.
But, they were not very heavy, and have become loose and worn
through the years. They also are rather large for the average collector,
often being eight feet long and nearly three feet wide. But, if you
have a place large enough, such a table would make a great dining
table!

LEGGED TABLES

The legged table has a leg at each corner, sometimes an extra leg or
two in the center if the piece has an exceptionally long top, and
sometimes extra legs which swing out to support wide leaves.

Let's start with a simple four-legged table. These vary in size from
rather small, often square, side tables to large dining tables. Small
tables can be found in nearly any period and style. They are not all
in museums. Many can be seen in antiques shops and at shows. Just
be sure the small table you are looking at is "of the period", meaning

DOWEL JOINT

SHIP LAP, HALF LAP OR RABBET

SPLINE JOINT

TONGUE AND GROOVE

it was made in the period of time its design would indicate. To make certain of this, know and trust the person from whom you are buying, or have someone authenticate it for you.

The construction of these tables is nearly the same through the periods. The main difference is in the design of the legs.

The earliest of the small tables had a one-board top. As time moved toward the 1800s, hardwood tops over 18 inches wide might have been made from two pieces of wood, often pegged together, or held together with a spline or tongue and groove joint. If the top of a simple table is two pieces, there is a good chance the boards only were butted together using no glue, pegs, or splines, and then nailed to the base.

In the mid-1800s, as wide hardwood boards became scarce, larger table tops, as well as other pieces of furniture, were made of several boards glued together. With the industrial revolution came the advent of doweling machines. By the late 1800s, in the cities at least, most boards were glued together and held in place with dowels or machine-cut tongue and groove joints. Splines, hand-made pegs, half laps, and hand-cut tongue and groove joints were used in country furniture until the end of the 19th century. Of course, some woodworkers still use these methods to join boards today in good, hand-made furniture.

In taverns around the country, small tables were used for serving patrons. These tables often were barely big enough for two to four people; and, they were made in great numbers. Today, we find small tables for sale in shops or at sales which are called *tap tables*. This is because these pieces were used in the taverns or bars which also were called "tap rooms", hence the name tap table. Other than in bars, small tables were used in homes for any number of purposes. Their size was good for nearly any room where a small table was needed.

Larger tables, which could accommodate more patrons, also were used in the early taverns. These usually were rather low, either rectangular or oblong, and on very simple bases. Such tables often are referred to as *tavern tables* for obvious reasons. Because of their size, they usually had stretchers.

DROP LEAF TABLES

Drop leaf tables are a way of getting more table when you need it without taking up valuable space. We find drop leaf tables from the Jacobean period, ca. 1650, through all of the other periods, right into contemporary furniture design. In the Jacobean period there were the gate leg and the butterfly drop leaves. Both are reproduced. So, if you are looking for something like this, be careful. After all,if you found one of these and it was "of the period", it would be over 300 years old; and, if it was right, it would be rather valuable.

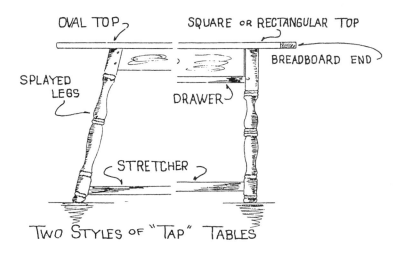

OVAL TOP

SQUARE or RECTANGULAR TOP

BREADBOARD END

SPLAYED LEGS

DRAWER

STRETCHER

Two Styles of "Tap" Tables

Then, we move into the William and Mary period with the use of walnut instead of the oak used in Jacobean pieces. Next, we have the Queen Anne period; here, you can find both four and six-legged drop leaf tables. This is also true in the later periods such as Chippendale, Hepplewhite, and Sheraton; whether formal or country, you will see either four or six-legged drop leaves, the number of legs depending upon the length and depth of the leaves. Occasionally, you may see a table with eight legs. These usually were rather formal in style, and more often English than American in manufacture.

When you see a four-legged drop leaf table, with a drawer in one end, and having rather narrow leaves, it usually is referred to as a *Pembroke*. This title is reserved for a more formal table rather than a pine or poplar country piece. The support which holds up these leaves when in use is most often a hinged piece of wood which fits into an opening in the skirt when not needed. The type of support used on country pieces may be the same, or it could be a simple, flat piece of wood which swings out of a hole cut into the top of the skirt and pivots on either a metal pin or wooden dowel. On some tables, usually from the greater New England area, the leaf support may be a flat piece of wood which pulls out of a small opening in the skirt. You can find these little drop leaf tables with no drawer, one drawer, or with two drawers, one at each end.

There are a few long, narrow-leaved tables around. They often are called *harvest* tables. These are very popular and are reproduced heavily. Do be especially careful if you are in the market for one.

When the leaves of a drop leaf are too long for simple supports, you will see a couple of extra legs, each tucked in next to one of the other table legs. Usually, you lift the leaf with your left hand and swing the extra, hinged leg out with your right. Very rarely, this all may be reversed. I can't help to wonder, the few times I've seen this, if maybe the woodworker who made the table was lefthanded!

Anyway, these extra legs usually are hinged to the skirt in a manner similar to that used for the supports of the smaller drop leaf tables. In both cases, the skirt is made up of two pieces, the inner one mortised and tenoned to the legs; the outer piece is nailed to the inner skirt. Most design features of these long-leafed tables are the same as their smaller counterparts; they just have longer leaves!

Another type of drop leaf table is the *swing* or *gate leg* table with four legs. This style usually is found in the Queen Anne and Chippendale periods, from 1720 to about 1780. Mostly, they were constructed of walnut and were made from New England, along the coast, south to the Virginia area. With this type of construction, two legs are fixed, or permanently attached to the frame while the other two legs are hinged, and swing out to support a leaf after it is lifted. Usually, these tables are small dining size; one of the advantages of only four legs is that there aren't as many legs to get in the way of diners!

LONG TABLES

Other than the harvest table, there were tables made which were so long that the maker had to add one or two legs in the center. This was to keep the center of the top from sagging. Such tables usually were used in large dining halls or in monasteries; they often are referred to as *refectory* tables and are very useful today for buffet dining or in a family room if the room is large enough! The extra legs should be of the same design as the other legs, and were built in the same manner as the rest of the table. Such tables are not really plentiful, but are worth searching out if you have the need and space for one.

In addition to the tables I've already mentioned, there were other long tables which were used for special occasions and/or certain purposes. There were tables made for industry such as *cutting* tables where material was laid out and cut for clothing, *library* tables which usually had a drawer or drawers built into the skirts, and any number of other tables. Most of these can be adapted for use in our homes today. There are a lot of long tables to be had; all you have to do is have the need for one. Then, find a table to fill that need. Or, if you find a table you just can't live without, you may have to develop a use for it!

FARM TABLES

Farm tables usually are heavier and more business-like than the other tables I've been talking about. A lot of them have removable tops; the top has a cleat at each end which fits over the outside of the base. There are holes at each corner of the cleat which go through it; and, there are corresponding holes in the base. To keep the top in place, a shaved wooden peg fits into each hole.

Also, many of these tables have fixed, or non-removable, tops. In these cases, the top is either screwed on from the bottom or nailed or pegged on from the top. Such tables usually were made of walnut, poplar, cherry, pine, or a combination of these woods. And, often they were painted. Much of the time, they have one or two drawers; and occasionally, there are three. The legs might be turned or square; and, the table may or may not have stretchers; but, the one thing they always are is heavy and strong!

They were used in the kitchen for all of the heavy, rough work which went with early farm life. Because of the use they generally received, the removable tops were replaced once in a while. If the top wasn't replaced, you can see all of the stains, knife cuts, etc. which make up the history of such a piece. These tables are great for the country kitchen; but, because they were made to work at and usually have little, if any, overhang, they do not make very good dining tables, unless someone replaces the narrow top with a wider one. Therefore, if a work table is easy to sit at, be careful!

HUTCH TABLES

As I wrote before, my farm background makes it difficult for me to call anything other than a rabbit coop a hutch. But, the definition of a hutch is "a chest, box, coffer, bin, coop or the like; as, a grain hutch; a rabbit hutch. To put away; hoard." So, I guess a tilt-top table with

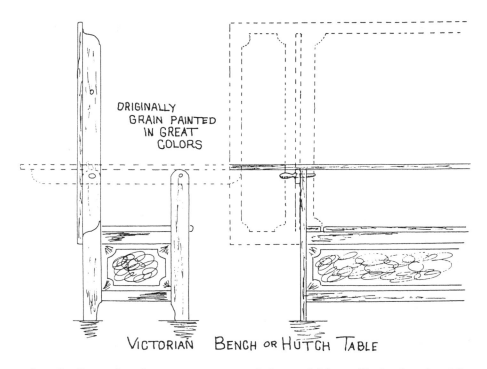

ORIGINALLY
GRAIN PAINTED
IN GREAT
COLORS

VICTORIAN   BENCH or HUTCH TABLE

a box built under the seat area certainly could be called a *hutch* table. Hutch tables have been around a long time and are very practical; you have a seat, a table, and a storage area. Most of the earliest have solid sides or ends with the bottoms of the hutch nailed into place. The fronts and backs of the hutch are dovetailed and nailed with the top either hinged with a metal hinge or a type of pintle hinge (wood pin). I also have seen lids which had no hinges; they just sat in place to protect the contents of the box.

In the early 1800s, these tables had panel ends; and, butt hinges were used. This style persisted into the late 1800s when most of them were grain painted to look like oak. Others were grained to look like oak with crotch mahogany panels painted on to resemble veneer inlay. Some of the paint jobs on these later tables are really nice. I feel if you find one painted, even if the paint is a little rough, which many are, you should try to save it if at all possible. I have seen a lot of these tables "refinished"; and, it upsets me because every time one is stripped, a piece of history goes down the drain; also, the remaining examples just get that much more expensive.

Around the end of the 19th century and into the early 20th century, there were tables made in factories which looked very much like the hutch tables I've just described. Often they had solid ends instead of panel ones; and, there wasn't a great deal of overhang to the top. The ends usually were two or three boards glued together, while the top might be made of five or six glued-up narrow boards. I saw an advertisement in an old magazine a few years ago showing these tables as "ironing tables". The irons and padding were stored in the box. When it was time to iron, the top was put down, covered with padding, and then was ready to use. When not needed, the top was tipped back; and, the proud owner had a seat which didn't take up much space. These tables can be found today; and, they look pretty old, especially since most were in or near a kitchen and were used by families with children. Your giveaway regarding age is the many board tops and the very short overhand on the ends. They are nice little tables; but, you can't pull a chair up to the ends, which makes them impractical for dining.

Bench, chair, and hutch tables are very popular; and, as I said, all are heavily reproduced; be careful. Look for natural wear and good proportions. Check every detail for raw wood, paint in the wrong places, wrong types of hardware, etc. These tables were made over a long period of time in nearly every part of the early Colonies. Some still are made today. Good, early, well-painted ones are rather scarce; however, there are some nice ones, both painted and refinished, still to be found. Just watch out for reproductions!

BENCH AND CHAIR TABLES

These tables are great if you have the space and setting for one. A *bench* or *chair* table doesn't take up a lot of room; but, the setting must be right for one to fit in. I have seen a lot of these; most are used as tables and only rarely as something on which to sit. It is hard to tell just when the ones we see today were first made. Some I've seen seem to date from the mid 18th century, while I know others which are early 20th century. There have been so many bench and chair tables made as copies, reproductions, and out and out fakes, that I would guess there may be as many reproductions as real ones for sale!

The difference between a bench table and a chair table is in their size, the chair table being much smaller. Both can be found in a variety of sizes and shapes with rectangular, round, or square tops. Typically, the sides of the base are one piece of wood, as wide as the "seat" board, cut out at the bottom to form feet, and cut out at the top

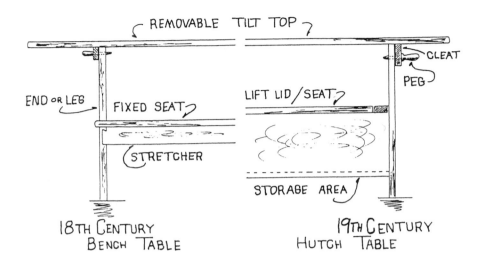

REMOVABLE TILT TOP

CLEAT

PEG

END or LEG

FIXED SEAT

LIFT LID / SEAT

STRETCHER

STORAGE AREA

18TH CENTURY
BENCH TABLE

19TH CENTURY
HUTCH TABLE

to form a sort of arm rest. The seat board usually is cut with tenons; and, the end pieces or sides have mortises cut into them. When these are fitted together, usually the tenons are wedged. This makes a rather tight-fitting joint. With some tables, strength was increased by adding an apron to the front and rear, just under the seat. These sometimes were dovetailed into the sides and other times just nailed into place. Still other bench or chair tables had drawers, one under the seat of a chair table and sometimes two or three drawers under a bench table seat. In early examples, the top should be made from one, two, or three boards, depending upon the size of the base it is on. The underside of the top has two cleats running across the grain of the wood, from edge to edge which usually have two, three, or four holes drilled near their ends that match holes drilled through the side pieces. Shaped pegs were placed through these holes to hold the top in place, whether it was down as a table, or up as a seat. These cleats may be dovetailed into the top, nailed to it, or pegged on with wooden pegs going through the top, into the cleats. Sometimes, you may see screws going through the top to hold the cleats in place. Generally, this is a later method, usually from the mid to late 1800s, the screws were added later to tighten things up a bit, or the top is a replacement. Many of the later examples had screws which were counter sunk and their holes then filled with round dowels; this is a giveaway that the piece isn't very old.

Most of the smaller, round-top, chair tables, made of pine, started life in New England, while the larger, rectangular-top bench tables,

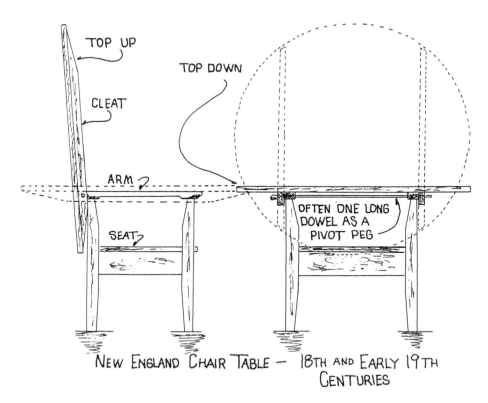

TOP UP

TOP DOWN

CLEAT

ARM

SEAT

OFTEN ONE LONG
DOWEL AS A
PIVOT PEG

NEW ENGLAND CHAIR TABLE — 18TH AND EARLY 19TH
CENTURIES

many made of poplar, are from Pennsylvania. This is very general; and, there are lots of exceptions. The majority of these tables were painted when they were made; however, few are left with their original paint intact. Those that are command rather high prices at antiques shows, shops, and sales. Because of this, you have to be very careful when buying a painted bench or chair table; they are fairly easy to paint; and, it's simple to make the paint look old. As I have written before, check for paint in cracks and joints where there shouldn't be any; and, be sure there is no paint over wear areas where it should have worn away through use.

CARD OR GAME TABLES

Most *card* or *game* tables are rather small compared to dining tables. However, the one thing that card tables have in common is that they almost always have a double top. This top is hinged with card

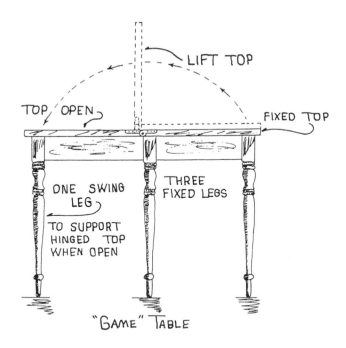

LIFT TOP

TOP OPEN

FIXED TOP

ONE SWING LEG

THREE FIXED LEGS

TO SUPPORT HINGED TOP WHEN OPEN

"GAME" TABLE

table hinges, which usually are brass, and are set into the edges of the two pieces of the top. Opened up, the top often is square or rectangular, and is supported either by a swing leg or by a method of turning the top so that it rests on the frame. The style of table having a fixed top and a swing leg for support usually has a drawer for cards, etc. The type with a turn top, which rests on the base frame, often only has storage space under the top for these items.

Game tables were made through many periods and styles, from Queen Anne to Empire. Examples can be found in a plain country style, often of pine or poplar; but, most of the game tables you'll see are in the more formal vein and were made of a hardwood, such as walnut, cherry, birch, maple, or mahogany. Generally, in the late Chippendale and Hepplewhite periods, many had nice veneering.

A card table makes a great hall table and is very handy as a server in a diningroom or as an occasional table in a bedroom. Of course, it also is great for playing cards or some other game!

THREE-PART DINING TABLES

Three part tables are not very popular today in most circles. They are just too big and too formal for the way most people live. These tables were made with one center section, often with drop leaves, and two end sections which usually had one leaf each. The periods in which these tables were produced ran from late Chippendale, early Hepplewhite to the middle of the Empire years. Most were made of dense mahogany and usually were rather formal in style. The center section could be used as a dining table when the size of the three pieces wasn't needed. The other two sections then would be placed against the wall to be used as servers. The way most of these tables were designed, they could be placed together with their leaves up or down. This gave quite a combination of possible sizes: all leaves down, one end piece with its leaf up, both end pieces with leaves up, one leaf up in the center section, both leaves up in the center section, and so on.

A lot of the three-section tables on the market are English; there is nothing wrong with that; just keep this in mind if you are planning to buy such a table; and, don't pay a premium for an "American" piece which wasn't made here. It might be hard to find a complete, three-section set. They often were separated through the years because their large size wasn't needed.

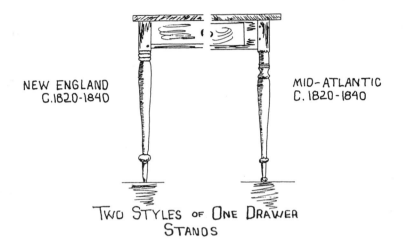

NEW ENGLAND
C.1820-1840

MID-ATLANTIC
C.1820-1840

Two Styles of One Drawer
Stands

STANDS

ONE-DRAWER STANDS

One of the most popular and useful antique stands is the one drawer example. It can be found in nearly any kind of finish from natural wood to painted. Stands are very useful in any room of a house, as "at home" in a kitchen as in a bedroom, useful in a bathroom or next to a sofa in a livingroom. A few have splayed legs; many have turned legs; and, some have square tapered legs. Most have square or rectangular tops, generally in the 18 to 24 inch range. A few of these stands may have round tops; and, occasionally you will see one with an oval top.

Most one-drawer stands date from the late 1700s to the late 1800s. If you search long and hard enough, you can find them dating from the late 1600s. The problem here, as with any other early, desirable item, is that they are scarce, expensive, and often faked. In most cases, the later stands are what people are looking for; and, even these are faked.

Often a drawer is added to a stand which never had one. Usually, it is fairly easy to tell if a drawer has been added. The first thing to check is the drawer itself. Is the front the same wood as the skirt of the stand? Are the finish and patina the same on the drawer front as on the rest of the piece? Turn the stand over and examine the drawer slides. Are they new? If so, why? A simple, inexpensive stand without a drawer can be turned into a nice, one-drawer stand rather easily by a good woodworker. If you are paying for a desirable one-drawer stand, be sure it started life as one.

TWO-DRAWER STANDS

Most of the two, and sometimes three, drawer stands are a bit fancier than the one-drawer examples. At least, it seems that way. It appears that there were a lot of one-drawer stands made in nearly every style and in most parts of the country. On the other hand, multi-drawer stands were made within a narrower time frame, starting around 1800 and being in vogue through the late Empire period. Examples can be found well into the late 1800s. There weren't very many made from pine with a real country look or feel. Many of the earlier multi-drawer stands have nice inlay; and, most were made of good-looking hard woods. A few even have drop leaves, which adds a whole different feeling; these look like miniature drop leaf tables, which they are, and are quite useful if you have the room and right decor for one.

Some of the Empire period stands are rather heavy looking; but, they look right with other pieces of the same period and are very well made, almost always of very pretty woods. These multi-drawer stands are quite useful. However, they look better in a bedroom, bath or livingroom than in a kitchen.

Some, especially the later ones, have a shelf connected to the lower part of the legs. Sometimes, this shelf is quite plain; other times, it has nice cut-outs along the front edge. Occasionally, a shelf may be found on a one-drawer stand, as well as a stand with no drawers.

STANDS WITH NO DRAWERS

There is a large range of styles of stands with no drawers which runs from the very early, primitive examples, to the fine candlestands of the Chippendale period, to the later, simple, square-legged stands of the late 1800s.

The most common and least expensive is the plain square-top stand which was made through several periods. Most have straight, square, tapered legs, sometimes splayed. Occasionally, there is a lip around the edge of the top. Generally, this indicates that the stand was used to serve tea. The lip helped keep the china from sliding off. This lip, by the way, also can be found on stands with one or more drawers. Stands without drawers usually are less expensive than the others I've mentioned; but, because they have no drawers, they are not as useful.

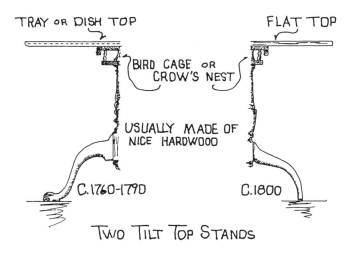

TWO TILT TOP STANDS

TRI-POD STANDS

This is another type of stand without a drawer. They can be found in several periods ranging from the mid 18th century well into the early 1900s. Tri-pod means three feet or legs. With these stands, the legs are fastened to the bottom of a central pedestal. Such stands are greatly reproduced, not so much as fakes, but because they are, and always have been, very popular. In fact, furniture makers still make them in great quantities!

Some people have a problem telling a stand which is forty or fifty years old from one which is a hundred and fifty years old. One way is that most of the early stands have a one-piece top, and certainly no more than two boards. Also, the legs are fitted into the bottom of the

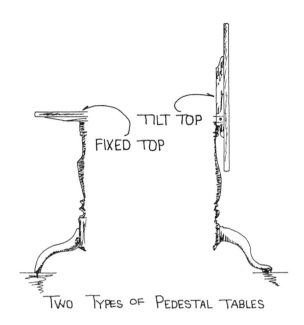

TWO TYPES OF PEDESTAL TABLES

pedestal by hand-cut dovetails, not dowelled into place which started sometime in the Victorian period. These dovetails should not be machine-cut; that would indicate a 20th century piece. Also, some of the later pedestals are made of glued up wood and not one piece as in the early ones.

There are many styles of the tri-pod stand, such as those with a very thin pedestal for a single candlestick, to those with rather large tops and heavier bases. This was used as a breakfast or tea table. There are tops which were fastened to the base very firmly; there are tops which tilt; and there are tops which tip and turn; the latter have a section under the top that is referred to as a *bird cage* or *crow's nest*.

Most of the tops on fixed top stands are round. Of course, there are exceptions. On the other hand, the tilt top stands can be found with round, oval, rectangular, and occasionally, square, hexagonal or octagonal tops. Many of the tilt top stands have inlay of some sort set into the top surface. Most stands with a bird cage or crow's nest have rather large, round tops; but, again, there are exceptions. The woods used in tri-pod stands usually are very pretty, such as walnut, cherry, mahogany, maple, including tiger or figured, and, once in a while, even bird's eye maple. I have seen many stands which were made with one wood for the top, a different wood for the pedestal,

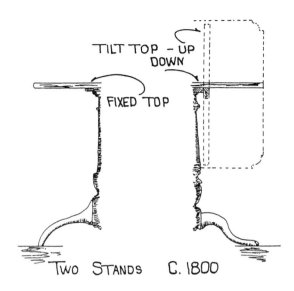

TILT TOP – UP
DOWN

FIXED TOP

TWO STANDS   C. 1800

and, at times, still another for the feet. However, the feet and pedestal often are of the same wood.

Most of the fixed top stands have one cleat running under the top, across the grain. The pedestal goes through the center of the cleat and usually is wedged on the top side of the cleat; then the cleat is screwed to the underside of the top. Some examples have the cleat nailed to the top. However, the cleat should not be glued; if it is, when the top moves back and forth, as wood will do because of humidity in the air, the top could split.

In the case of the tilt-top stands, there should be two cleats, screwed to the underside of the top, one on each side of a block which is fastened to the top of the pedestal. At one end of the block, there usually are two dowels or pegs which protrude and fit into holes in the cleats. On the other end of the block is a locking device of some sort to keep the top from tipping when it shouldn't. This lock usually is brass; but, I have seen some which were wooden turn knobs.

The bird cage on the tip and turn stands is made of two squares of wood held together with four turnings, one at each corner. There is a hole in the center of each square block which is slightly larger than the diameter of the top of the pedestal. The cage fits over the end of the pedestal which has a slot in it that is located between the two blocks of the cage. A wedge fits into this slot and keeps the cage in place while still allowing it to turn. The top block of the cage has dowels or pegs very similar to the tilt-top stand block. These round pieces of wood fit into cleats which run across the grain on the underside of the top. The cleats then are screwed to the top.

Stands with tiltable tops were and are very handy; when the stand isn't in use or if you need space, you can tilt the top and fit the stand into a corner, getting it out of the way. Most stands are very attractive with their tops tipped.

Dished tops, also called *tray tops* or *pie crust* tops, are much sought after and generally considered "top of the line", as far as tri-pod stands or tables are concerned. They weren't made for too many years in this country, and usually are of mahogany or walnut. Most of these stands have tilt tops; and, some have tip and turn tops. Because of their size, many are as large as three feet in diameter, they're considered tea tables or tea stands. Again, the addition of a lip, no matter what it is called, helped keep things, such as good china, on the table top.

Since these stands are fairly rare, some faking is done. I have seen a few which had the top sanded down in the central area, therefore leaving an edge or lip around the circumference. If it is flat, and made of wood which is thick enough, this can be done fairly easily by a good woodworker. If the top seems to be over-finished and too "pretty" for the rest of the stand, be suspicious. In a case where the center of the top has been sanded, the top wouldn't show any age, and may have a much different look than the rest of the table; there are some nice dish-top stands on the market. But, there also are some fakes. Just be careful.

A lot of these stands are English; and, sometimes, it is very hard to tell English from American ones. If in doubt, compare the style of the pedestal and feet with known American examples shown in reference books; and, have someone who really knows period furniture examine it for you. There certainly is nothing wrong with a nice, early, English tea table. However, if you are paying for a period American piece, that's what you should be getting.

As I briefly mentioned earlier, another fixed top tri-pod stand is the one made for holding a single candle, the candlestand. Of course, any stand can hold a candlestick; however, the larger ones also could hold other household items. But, the small-topped candlestand isn't large enough to hold much except a single candle or a small vase of flowers. The earliest of these are very primitive; some date to the late 1600s or early 1700s. In the mid 18th century, more refinements were adopted; and, the candlestand was very pretty, though small. These stands still are made today; but, it isn't difficult to tell the newer ones from the early pieces; the workmanship, materials, color, and finish are giveaways. Also, as mentioned before, the pedestals in the newer pieces are glued up.

A great deal can be told about the date of a stand by the shape of its legs and feet, as well as its top. Of course, just looking at a stand, taking in the top, pedestal, legs, and feet, will give you an idea of its age. That is if it hasn't been reworked or faked.

As for the pedestal, if it is original and has not been re-turned on a lathe at a later date, it should be a bit out of round; with your hand or a pair of calipers, check the diameter of the turning. If it is out of round, it most likely is "of the period"; however, if it is perfectly round, something is wrong. Why hasn't it shrunk?

Now, to the tops and legs. This information is rather general; but, it will help you determine the age within a few years; and, that often is close enough. Legs which come out of the bottom of the pedestal, turn down, and then turn out again are the earliest. They usually end in either a ball and claw foot in the earlier, larger stands or in a form of pad foot, in the smaller and often later stands of the Chippendale period. Around 1790, the styles changed; the legs came out of the pedestal and turned down and out, usually ending bluntly on the floor with no real feet, except on a few Hepplewhite examples which have a bit of a knob at the bottom just where the foot touches the floor. The Sheraton legs do not have this bit of a foot. Some tripod stands of the Empire period had casters.

Tops generally were round on the earlier, small stands; once in a while, there might be an oval or octagonal top in the Chippendale period; but, most were round. Occasionally, through this period, you may see a stand with a gallery. With few exceptions, these are English. If someone tries to sell you one which is supposed to be American-made, be careful. Around 1790, the start of the Hepplewhite period, many shapes of tops started to appear. Most of these shapes still are made today. Such pieces really aren't fakes; they're just so popular that furniture manufacturers keep making them.

Newly manufactured stands are easy to spot. The tops are either glued up using several pieces of wood or are a type of plywood with the edges filled in to look like solid wood. You usually can detect this type of top. Also, the pedestals on such stands almost always are glued up; and, the glue lines are fairly easy to see.

There are fakes, however. And, if you're looking at a nice stand of the Hepplewhite or Sheraton periods with interesting cut-outs at the corners of the top, be sure to check carefully. Most of these stands had round, oval, or rectangular tops; there is little which can be done with the round or oval top; but, the rectangular one is easy to change from "plain" to "fancy". If you see a stand that has nice cut-outs at the corners of the top, examine them carefully to be sure they are original. A stand with a plain top is not as expensive as one with nice cut-outs. Look at the edges of the cut area to see if the wood looks as old as the other surfaces; this is important when considering a piece like this. Watch for unusual tool marks and/or raw-looking wood. Even if the stand recently has been refinished, raw, new-looking wood is hard to hide.

With this type of stand, another favorite thing for fakers is to add inlay. A lot of stands in these periods had inlay; some of it was really great, with complex designs like eagles and flowers, or as simple as a plain piece of wood, in a contrasting color. It often is hard to tell if the inlay is new or old. Originally, it would have been set in by hand; but, a good faker also would set inlay by hand, using the right woods, which makes detection rather difficult. The best thing to do is examine the inlaid area under a magnifying glass; look for modern glue in the joints, as well as traces of glue in the pores of the wood surrounding the inlaid area. An otherwise plain-top table can be enhanced, and its value raised, with the addition of nice inlay. So, if you are looking at a stand with inlay, check it out as well as possible.

There is still another type of candlestand; this one is called a *torchere* and usually is from England. They are very nice, rather tall, about three feet high, and have very small, usually dished tops. Generally, you see them in matched pairs; however, I'm sure many pairs have been broken up through the years. These little stands are very nice, and are great for holding a special candlestick.

WASHSTANDS

A lot of things are called washstands, from plain flat-top stands, flat-top stands with cut-outs for washbowls, corner stands, some without cut-outs, some with, and small case pieces, usually with either a lift top or doors on the lower section to hide the wash bowl and other items used in conjunction with it. Washstands also are called *basin stands;* most have a *splash board.* If it is a corner stand, the splash

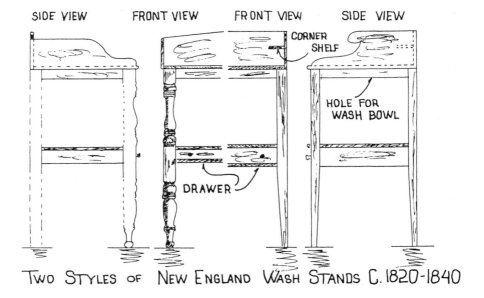

SIDE VIEW   FRONT VIEW   FRONT VIEW   SIDE VIEW

CORNER SHELF

HOLE FOR WASH BOWL

DRAWER

Two Styles of New England Wash Stands C. 1820-1840

board is on the two sides which make up the back; these boards helped keep the walls from being splashed when someone was washing. If the stand isn't a corner one, the splash board would be higher in the back and taper down from the back to the front along each side.

There isn't much information on washstands, or anything else regarding bathing, as far as furniture goes, before the late Chippendale period. Some washstands date from about 1780; but, most were made starting around 1790. The majority of washstands were made before the 1830s; after that, they became case pieces which totally hid the wash bowl, etc.

Washstands made from 1790 to 1830 generally had a shelf, often with a drawer, somewhere below the middle. The top had a cut-out area which held the bowl; and, the pitcher sat in the bowl. The other items were kept on the shelf. Some of the splash boards were rather high; and, usually, they had a small corner shelf attached.

These stands generally were of very fine woods and beautifully made. Many were made to fit into a corner; this kept them out of the way when they were not in use. Some had handles cut into the splash board so they could be moved easily. Such stands can be used today to hold flowers or some other light-weight decoration. Rather than have the hole filled or a new top put on one of these stands, fit it with a bowl and use it as it is. Or, put a piece of wood the size of the top over the hole. This helps the piece hold its value better than altering it would, even if it isn't useful with the bowl cut-out. Such stands usually are so simple in design that they fit fairly well into almost any home.

About 1830 or so, up to the late 19th century, there were wash-stands made; but, they were not as classy as the earlier ones. Some were case pieces, with storage under the lid and/or behind doors; and, some were just simple stands with a shelf underneath. During the mid to late Victorian period, such stands often had dowels on ei-ther side for towels. These later ones usually were made of pine or poplar. Most of these do not have a bowl cut-out, and, therefore, are easier to use.

I don't know of much faking as far as washstands are concerned, except to replace the tops which have holes in them with solid pieces of wood.

If you are suspicious, look for raw edges, wrong colors, and other telltale marks along the edges. Look for new nails and modern glue at the joints. If the job was good and the piece isn't over-priced, don't worry about it; a stand like this is more useful with the top solid.

SEWING STANDS OR TABLES
(*also called* WORK STANDS)

Sewing stands may be a bit fancy for the person decorating with country furniture; however, many of them still are quite useful in a home where someone sews. Most sewing stands have several draw-ers which can be used today to hold the items they were made to hold—scissors, thread, thimbles, needles, etc.

Some sewing stands also have a bag hanging from the underside. These are called *bag-stands* or *bag tables*. The silk bag held material and things which needed mending. Not many of the bags survived the rigors of regular use. I would think a bag-stand with a replaced bag would be OK; of course, if the bag is original, that is great! Often, a worn out silk bag was replaced with a bag made from dif-ferent material.

These sewing stands, both the bag type and the non-bag type, usu-ally were made of fine woods; and, they were nicely finished. Most date from about 1790 to 1850. Some of these stands were grain-painted and are rather plain. The plainer ones are hard to find, but well worth the search.

Another piece of furniture which held sewing paraphernalia is the *Martha Washington* sewing table or stand which seems to be purely American. These stands got their name because Mrs. Washington was supposed to have used one at Mount Vernon.

This type of stand was made from the Hepplewhite to the Empire periods and can be found with square-tapered legs, turned legs, or a center pedestal with either three or four feet. The leg style, of course, changed with the period in which the stand was made. The style of the sewing stand itself, not the legs, is what makes it a Martha Washington. The case, or body, generally is oval in shape. These stands have a section at each end and a center section, usually with drawers, while the end sections are sort of "wells" to hold material and things to be mended. They have either one lid which covers the top and hinges from the rear, or lids over each well which lift while the center section remains fixed.

There are a lot of reproduction Martha Washington stands on the market; as a matter of fact, I have seen more reproductions of these than real ones. One thing to watch for when looking at this type of stand is the use of plywood for drawer bottoms and the back. If you examine carefully, you can spot a reproduction. Such stands are very handy, useful pieces of furniture if they fit in with your decor. The drawers and wells hold lots of things. Of course, they also are quite useful as sewing stands!

BOOK STANDS

These stands generally are English; and, I only mention them here because I'm talking about stands. Most of them are made with a center pedestal, and have a revolving upper section which holds books. There also are book stands which are little more than shelves. But, they are very nicely made. These often have a drawer under a lower shelf. They date from the late 1700s to the early 1800s, both the pedestal and the shelf types. Secretaries and built-in shelves seem to have taken their place!

SHAVING STANDS

Again, most of these items are English; however, there are some American examples, especially the later ones made during the Empire period. These stands were made to sit on a dressing table or chest of drawers, and, were for gentlemen who used them for dressing and/or shaving. The mirror section usually could pivot; and, they often had from one to three drawers in them. Most were made of fine woods and were well made, rarely painted, and generally rather formal.

MUFFIN STANDS

These tiered stands usually are English; however, there are a few which are American-made. They generally were used with a tea service.

MUSIC STANDS

These were made in America, Europe, and England. They date from the 17th century in Europe and England, and appeared in America in the mid to late 18th century. After the 1840s, they were not as nice; and, toward the end of the 1800s, metal ones were being made.

URN STANDS

Usually English, these stands were made from the mid to late 18th century to the Empire period. They were used to hold urns; and, sometimes, they were used in England as part of the tea service.

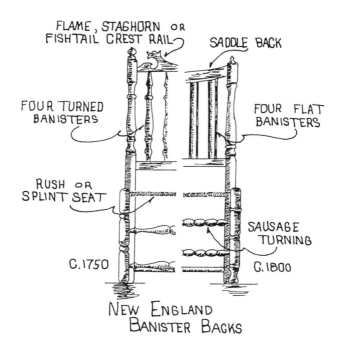

FLAME, STAGHORN OR
FISHTAIL CREST RAIL

SADDLE BACK

FOUR TURNED
BANISTERS

FOUR FLAT
BANISTERS

RUSH OR
SPLINT SEAT

SAUSAGE
TURNING

C.1750

C.1800

NEW ENGLAND
BANISTER BACKS

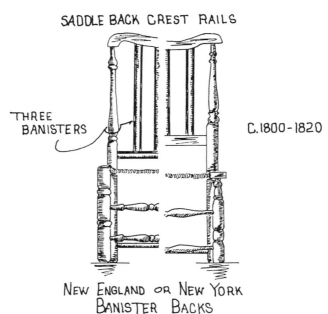

SADDLE BACK CREST RAILS

THREE
BANISTERS

C.1800-1820

NEW ENGLAND OR NEW YORK
BANISTER BACKS

CHAIRS

BANISTER-BACK CHAIRS

Banister, also spelled *bannister,* apparently was corrupted from the word "baluster". The definition of baluster is "a small column supporting a railing or balustrade"; and, the definition of banister is "a column or rail in a balustrade". Since a banister-back chair has columns between the end posts which run from the bottom rail to the crest rail, I guess these columns should be called balusters, which is the case in England. Most of the folks I know prefer banister. So, that is how I'll refer to these dignified chairs.

Banister-back chairs seem to have evolved from the English *cane chairs,* so called because they have cane seats and center sections in their backs. They were made in England from about 1660 to the early 1700s. They seem to have become popular in America around 1690 or so, but remained popular for only 20 to 30 years. The chair designers and makers in this country came up with the banister-back style around 1700. It became very popular, so popular, in fact, that this style of chair was made continually in one form or another well into the 1800s; some date from as late as 1825. Banister-backs also were made in England from around 1700 to about 1750, but not to the extent to which they were made on this side of the Atlantic.

There are many styles of banister-back chairs; however, they all have one thing in common: the banisters. Some have three banisters; some have five; and some arm chairs have six. However, most chairs have four. The banisters usually were turned on a lathe. The chairmaker would glue two pieces of wood together with a piece of paper between them. He then would turn the banister, usually in the same design as the end posts. Next, he would split the two pieces of wood apart at the paper line, clean off remnants of glue and paper, and, therefore, have two half turnings.

Sometimes, the banisters were not turned in the same style as the end posts; and, other times they were not turned at all. Usually, the turned banisters were put into the bottom and crest rails with their flat sides toward the seat; however, sometimes, the turned sides were toward the seat. The latter is not very comfortable; and, banister-backs need all the help they can get in relation to comfort! This reversed banister style seems to be more common in chairs made in Connecticut and occasionally, in chairs from England.

Banister-backs have a variety of feet. You can find them with Spanish feet, tapered turned feet, nice ball turnings, square feet, and simple turned feet. Most are side chairs; but, there are many examples of banister-back armchairs. The end posts usually have square, unturned areas where the arms are attached. Most banister-backs are made of maple which is a fine wood for turning and carving. You may find these chairs in "old red" or natural; but, most are in black paint. Other than some obviously new paint, I don't remember ever seeing a banister-back in any other colors.

Most of these chairs were made in New England, many in Massachusetts and Connecticut, and a few in Rhode Island and New Hampshire; however I have seen examples from Pennsylvania, New York, and New Jersey, as well as some from England. The styles are very similar; but, most of the Spanish foot and plain foot examples came from New England, as did most of the chairs with *sausage turned* stretchers, while most banister-backs with bolder front stretcher turnings came from Pennsylvania. There are exceptions, since styles were copied then, as they are now!

The crest rails of banister-back chairs show a lot of imagination in design. There is the plain *saddle-back,* the slightly fancier double curve, the more exciting *flame-back* which also is called the *stag horn* and the *fishtail,* the nice *heart-and-crown,* and the very elaborate crest rail with carved scroll work. You can see the influence of the earlier cane chairs in the crest rails of some of the early banister-backs.

While the cane chairs obviously had cane seats, the banister-backs mostly had seats made from rush. Rush is cat-tails, gathered, dried, then soaked, and woven into a seat. If the seat is quite old, it might be hard to tell if it is original or not. Although most of these chairs had rush seats, there were some with splint. These often were from a later date, but not always.

There are a few examples of child-size banister-backs. I have seen them only in photos, museums, and house restorations. I never have owned or restored one of these little gems. They usually are a small version of the adult size; however, there also are high chairs, which, of course, have no adult counterpart. The child or youth chair is often in a little rougher condition than the adult chair. Considering the occupant, you can understand why!

If you are in the market for a banister-back, there are a few things to watch out for. First of all, if it seems to be freshly painted, be careful; you can't tell what the paint may be hiding. Like many other types of chairs, the banister-back has a couple of weak spots; one in particular is the area of the rear post where the seat supports enter. This is an inherently weak spot in many chairs. It often is repaired, sometimes well and sometimes only temporarily; new paint could be hiding either kind or repair. You should know if it has been repaired and what kind of repair was done.

We own a very nice, flame-back, banister-back in an old red wash under red paint which has a great repair as far as imagination and charm go, but not a good repair in a professional sense. It probably was the best job the owner could do at that point in time. Obviously, the chair was considered valuable enough to be fixed. At that weak spot, there is a crack, not all the way through. Someone cut out a small channel and set in an oval piece of metal with holes in it. Then, the metal was screwed into place, one screw above the crack, one below. Whoever did it did not have any training in furniture repair; but, that person did the best he could with what was available at the time. And, he had enough of an aesthetic mind to recess the piece of metal so that it is flush with the wood surface! I was going to remove that metal patch and repair the chair professionally. However, my wife convinced me that it was such an honest repair and part of the chair's history, it should be left as is. When you see repairs such as this, they should be left alone, if at all possible, and enjoyed for what they are—honest, sincere repairs.

Another weak spot on a banister-back is at the crest rail where the banisters fit in. Often, due to pressure from many backs, the thin area between the mortice and the back of the rail breaks out. This can be repaired by a professional, or, if you are handy, by you. What must be done is one of two things—if the thin area is cracked, it may need only regluing. If, however, it is a bad break, you may have to set in a new piece of wood. This could end up as a major repair. So, if you are not handy and/or knowledgeable in furniture repairs, have a professional do it. This is, of course, another reason to question fresh paint on a banister-back. Also, it is an area to check, especially if there is new paint on the chair you are thinking of buying.

One way to check for repainting is to examine the seat material where it comes into contact with the legs. Also, look for paint over wear areas such as stretchers and the upper part of the front legs where they protrude above the seat.

When looking for a banister-back chair, one thing to watch out for is a reworked crest rail. If the crest rail is carved, check to be sure the carving isn't newer than the rail! It is easy to change a rather plain rail into a nicely carved one. Of course, this would make the chair more valuable on the market. So, if there is any carving, examine it closely. Also, watch for any tell-tale marks along the edges which may indicate a re-shaped crest rail.

Another thing which is done with banister-back chairs is the changing of the banisters. A rather plain chair with flat, unturned banisters can be made more exciting and a lot more expensive by removing those banisters and replacing them with nice turned ones; this isn't a big job for a woodworker, especially if the chair is damaged in the first place, and is already apart or broken. I have examined banister-back chairs which seemed to have both the crest rail and the banisters replaced.

By replacing these items, you could totally change the look and value of a banister-back. The crest rail and banisters can be replaced without removing or damaging the original seat. You might not expect these replacements if the seat looks original. But, do be careful; it can be done.

If a banister-back has been repainted and there have been repairs made, that's fine, as long as the work is good, and as long as you know it before you buy the chair. It's not fine if you have paid top dollar for an "untouched" banister-back chair!

COUNTRY QUEEN ANNE CHAIRS

The Queen Anne period in American furniture generally is considered to be from about 1720 to 1760, overlapping the William and Mary period in the beginning, and being overlapped by the Chippendale period in the later years. This style of furniture originated in England and has a very obvious Dutch influence.

I see no reason to spend a lot of time and space here going into the details of the really great Queen Anne chairs which many of us will never see, and fewer of us ever own. To learn more about these, I would suggest visits to some good museums and house restorations,

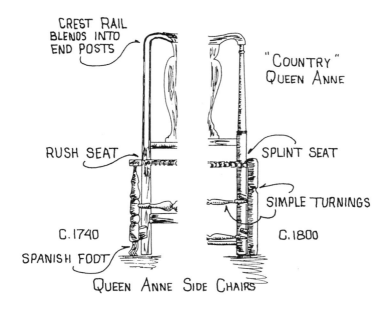

CREST RAIL
BLENDS INTO
END POSTS

"COUNTRY"
QUEEN ANNE

RUSH SEAT

SPLINT SEAT

SIMPLE TURNINGS

C. 1740

C. 1800

SPANISH FOOT

QUEEN ANNE SIDE CHAIRS

or at least a look at the photos in good reference books, most of which can be found in libraries and in book stores specializing in publications about antiques, especially furniture.

I could go on for pages, talking about the beautiful, more formal, Philadelphia and Baltimore chairs with their wonderful ball-and-claw feet, their nicely carved shells, and the great splats; but, I feel the time spent here would be more educational if I stick to the styles and types I know best, and the ones you are more likely to come in contact with—the early Dutch or country [rural] Queen Anne chairs dating from about 1720 to the early 1800s.

Obviously, a chair dating from around 1800 isn't a Queen Anne piece. However, the chair style was so popular that it carried on into the next period or two after the general design of Queen Anne had passed on in most other forms of furniture. These chairs generally are referred to as *country* or *rural* Queen Anne and sometimes *Dutch* chairs, regardless of when they were made. You also will hear them called *fiddle-backs*, *Dutch splat-backs*, or *York* chairs. The Dutch or Queen Anne chairs I will be telling you about developed from the English cane chairs, as did bannister-backs, around 1710 to 1720.

The first Queen Anne chairs came out of New England, later followed by ones made in New York, New Jersey, and Pennsylvania. Other styles, similar to these, also were made in other areas in the later years.

The earliest of the country Queen Annes had Spanish feet, a carryover from the William and Mary cane chairs, a yoke-shaped top rail, a solid splat in the center, and nice continuous lines flowing from the end posts to the top rail. Also, like the cane chairs, the splat ended in a bottom rail with space between the seat and its rail, not into the back of the seat as with the later Queen Anne chairs.

These early chairs have a nicely turned, bulbous stretcher in the front, and either rectangular or turned side and rear stretchers. The chairs with rectangular stretchers have one on each side and one in the rear, while those with turned stretchers may have one or two on each side, often very nicely turned, and one in the rear, usually turned to resemble the side stretchers. The end posts or stiles either are straight or *spoon-back* shaped (side view). The spoon-back versions, with fancy side stretchers, really are quite pretty and graceful. Also, each style is very light, both in weight and feeling. As far as I can tell, most chairs of this type were made in New England, mostly in Connecticut. However, a few came from Massachusetts and New Hampshire.

The next design in the evolution of country Queen Annes is the appearance of Dutch or pad feet and turned rear posts or stiles. Chairs with these features were made in the Albany area, as well as in New York City. This style started around 1725 and was so popular that it continued to after 1800.

These chairs have nicely turned front legs, ending in pad feet, usually well turned end posts or stiles, and one bulbous turning in the front. I always have seen them with two stretchers on each side and one in the rear. However, some with only one side stretcher may exist. The side stretchers are very simple, not fancy like the earlier Connecticut chairs. It appears that after these chairs became popular, chairmakers in southern Connecticut also started making them. Such chairs with their pad feet often are referred to as York chairs.

Because of the long time period in which so many rural pieces were made, it is very difficult, if not sometimes nearly impossible, to put an exact date on a piece of furniture. It is much safer, and wiser, to say that a piece is of a certain style or period than to give a definite date. This philosophy is most important when dealing with these country Queen Anne chairs, especially since they were made in one form or another from about 1720 to well into the 1800s. In fact, some good reproductions of the New York style still are made today.

In the earliest of these chairs, the rear posts or stiles were shaped from squares of wood with the crest rail nicely blended in. The next type had turned rear posts with the crest rail resting on them, protruding a bit at each end, as well as turned front legs with shaped pad feet. Now, we come into still a later type, starting about 1730 or so, and continuing, again, well into the early years of the 1800s. This style has both front and rear turnings. As a matter of fact, except for the crest rail, splat, and bottom rail, all of the members are turned. These chairs are light in weight, pleasant to look at, and rather durable. Also, they have been made for so long, mostly in New England, that they are fairly plentiful and not overly expensive.

The main problem a buyer might have is in telling which chairs were made in the early part of the period and which in the later years. The earlier ones should cost more. As with any piece of furniture, check all areas of the chair for telltale signs of modern tools. Once convinced the piece is not a reproduction, then start examining other details. Generally, the earliest Dutch or country Queen Anne examples are the ones with the Spanish feet; next the pad feet were popular; then, the chairs with completely turned front legs came into vogue. There are exceptions; and, of course, these styles overlapped in years, with each style being made for many years. So, you need to do more than just look at the style to figure out a date. The best, but certainly not fool-proof, way to get some idea of age is to examine the overall chair. The earliest Spanish-foot Queen Annes usually are lighter in look and feel than later examples in the same style. Aesthetically, they are much more pleasing. The earliest New York style chairs with their pad feet are nicely done and lovely to look at, not as burly as the later versions.

Country Queen Anne chairs usually were painted black. A few were red; and some were black over red. Any chair in a different color or a "natural" finish most likely has had something done to its original finish. Always be careful of repainted pieces. What repairs may be hidden by the new paint? Also, the wood in these chairs should be maple; the splat may be pine or poplar; but, the rest of the chair almost always was made of maple, whether the piece is from New England, New York, or Pennsylvania. The seats usually were of rush. However, some of the seats may have been splint.

Some of these chairs were made in the New Jersey and Pennsylvania area, especially the later versions. It is difficult to tell them from their New York counterparts; but, the New Jersey and

Pennsylvania chairs often have heavier legs and bolder front stretcher turnings than the New York examples. Also, some of them have nice cabriole legs which is rare in the New England chairs of this period. However, I feel that unless you have some pretty strong evidence, you would be wise to assume a country Queen Anne was made either in New England or New York.

The more obviously Pennsylvania styles are the more formal pieces which followed the introduction of the first Dutch or country Queen Anne chairs of the early 1700s. Keep in mind, most of the folks who first settled in New Jersey and especially in Pennsylvania were of Germanic background and were not as influenced by the English styles as the New England settlers; so, their furniture didn't reflect the changes in England the way their northern neighbors' pieces did. This is more noticeable in country furniture than in "high style" examples which were made in the Philadelphia, Albany, New York City, and Baltimore areas. As I mentioned earlier, these more formal chairs are very nice, and, in most cases, quite elegant. And, they are much easier to tell from New England chairs than the country pieces I am talking about.

Most of these are side chairs; but, there are a few armchairs of the country Queen Anne style to be found. The arms usually rest on the top of the extended front legs. But, occasionally, the arms may be supported by a spindle running from the top stretcher to the arm, generally notched at the seat for added strength. The latter usually is considered a Pennsylvania design; but, again, not always. Quite often, the New York and New England armchairs have more rounded arms than the Pennsylvania and New Jersey chairs whose arms are flatter.

Country Queen Anne chairs generally are plain enough that they can be used in nearly any simple setting. Also, there are plenty of them on the market; so, they are fairly easy to find, and are fun to search out, trying to find matching chairs. A set of four or five side chairs with one or two armchairs would make a nice setting around a plain, pine table.

WINDSOR CHAIRS

Volumes have been written about *Windsor* chairs. Nearly every book about antique furniture has something to say regarding these

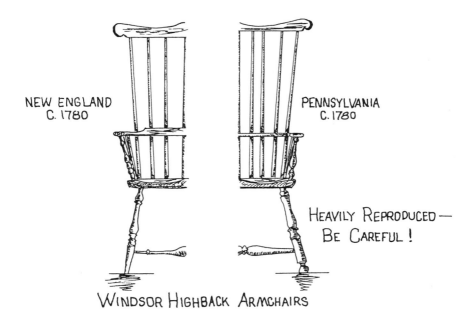

NEW ENGLAND
C. 1780

PENNSYLVANIA
C. 1780

HEAVILY REPRODUCED —
BE CAREFUL !

WINDSOR HIGHBACK ARMCHAIRS

very popular items. The whole thing seems to have started around Windsor Castle in England about 1700. Apparently, the first chairs were made by wheelwrights or turners rather than by cabinetmakers. Many of the early English Windsors have pierced slats in the centers of the backs with turned spindles on either side which suggest wheel spokes. However, the American Colonists carried the Windsor to its ultimate development, producing a chair of the utmost comfort, strength, lightness, and ease of manufacture.

The first American Windsors were made in the Philadelphia area after 1725; by around 1760, they were most popular and very common. They appeared in many variations of the basic styles such as comb-back, fan-back, hoopback, and bowback, and usually were made with a combination of woods. The saddle-shaped seat generally was of thick pine or poplar, and, sometimes, but rarely, made of birch or chestnut. The bent members usually were of hickory or white oak, and occasionally, ash. The turnings almost always were made of maple. Generally, these chairs were painted; however, sometimes, they were left raw or unfinished.

Windsors are very sought after and have become rather expensive; therefore, when you see one or two or a set which you feel you cannot live without, check them very carefully. As I said earlier, these

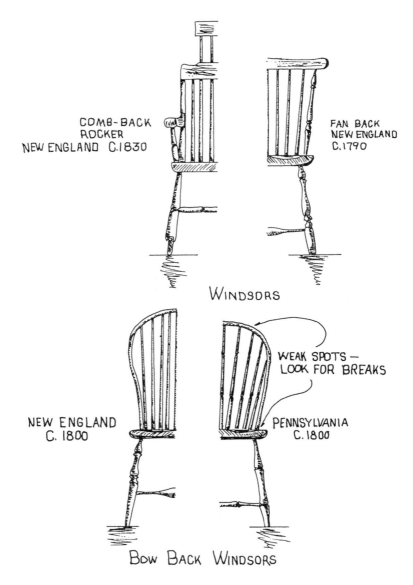

COMB-BACK
ROCKER
NEW ENGLAND C.1830

FAN BACK
NEW ENGLAND
C.1790

WINDSORS

WEAK SPOTS —
LOOK FOR BREAKS

NEW ENGLAND
C. 1800

PENNSYLVANIA
C.1800

BOW BACK WINDSORS

chairs have been made in this country since around 1725, and still are
being made. Some of the late 19th and early 20th century reproductions are being sold as "early". Because they are exact, hand-made
copies of 18th and early 19th century Windsors, even some of the
new, ten to twenty year old, chairs with a bit of aging and a lot of
paint are hard to tell from the early ones.

The first and most obvious thing to look for is a glued-up seat. Until the mid 1800s, Windsor chair seats were made from one thick, solid, piece of wood, not two or more pieces glued together. Be sure to check for machine marks on the bottom of the seat. By 1860 to 1870, many of the chairmakers were using machinery to smooth the lumber from which plank seats were made, rather than relying upon the old, time-consuming method of hand planing. Of course, a 20th century reproduction could have a one-board seat with a hand planed bottom; because of this, whether the seat is truly old or not is something you will have to determine by examining the other details of the chair.

While on the subject of seats, most of the early Windsors you will encounter should have a softwood, pine or poplar seat; as I mentioned before, a seat occasionally was made of a hardwood. But, this is the exception, not the rule. However, when the *firehouse* Windsor came along toward the end of the 1800s, the seats almost always were of a hardwood. Such Windsors were mass-produced, are very comfortable, and are quite affordable. They were bought in large quantities and used in firehouses, bars, restaurants, hotels, etc. Today, they can be found all over for a variety of prices, ranging from inexpensive to ridiculous! To the untrained eye, some of these chairs look a bit like their earlier counterparts. The best way to tell the difference is to know what each type looks like.

There are some antique furniture books which are devoted totally to 18th and early 19th century Windsors. Examine the pictures, trying to memorize what they look like. Then, search out a firehouse Windsor, either a photo or the real thing; you will be able to see the differences.

The seats in firehouse Windsors are rather flat compared to those of the earlier chairs which usually have nice saddle shapes. Also, most of these later chairs have *box stretchers* with two stretchers, one over the other, between each leg, while many of their earlier counterparts have an "H" stretcher arrangement.

Most of the firehouse Windsors have arms, some of which look like those of the early bowback, knuckle-arm chairs. But, the legs of a later Windsor have no class; they do not have the rake or angle of those on early chairs. Instead, they usually sit out very close to the edge of the seat, as in an English Windsor. The over-all chair has no grace and very little style; most firehouse Windsors seem bulky, as if everything is too big! They are, however, very comfortable. If you don't want to spend money on reproductions and/or can't afford to buy early Windsors, the firehouse chairs are rather nice in an informal setting. Just be sure you know what you are getting and pay accordingly.

There are a lot of chairmakers turning out reproduction Windsors today. Some of these 20th century chairs are obviously reproductions, while some are very well done, made by hand, using the old methods. These are the ones to watch out for. There is a general grace and lightness in the early Windsors which you usually do not find in the reproductions. However, unless you can set the two types side by side and study each, it sometimes is quite difficult to recognize a good reproduction.

The best thing to do is search out known reproductions. Go to a shop that sells them. Examine them very carefully and remember every detail which would indicate what they are. Then, with that information firmly etched in your mind, examine some authentic Windsors. Some of the differences are very subtle; but, they are there.

By about 1800 to 1820, the bamboo type turnings were catching on for Windsor chairs. And, by the 1820s, box stretchers and bamboo turnings had pretty well taken over as the design used by most of the chairmakers of the day. At around the same time, arrow-back chairs, which also are a type of Windsor, started to appear. As you can see, by this time, every plank-seat chair with turned legs and spindles was, and still is, called a Windsor, regardless of its age. I have a hard time calling all of these different types of chairs Windsors. To me, the real Windsor chairs stopped with the Sheraton styles of the early 1800s. These Sheraton chairs usually are found with bamboo turnings, and, like the earlier Windsors, nearly always have softwood seats. The earliest Sheraton examples are well made, and have nice, delicate turnings. They also have been reproduced by the thousands, the later ones getting heavier and less graceful. All of the information I've given you regarding reproductions applies to this style of chair as well.

Some tips on identifying an early Windsor are easy to remember, and apply to all styles of chairs made before 1800. The long, light spindles of the early examples had to be made by hand, or a slow, man-powered lathe. You may see some slight variations in the size, not the style, of them in the earliest chairs. However, spindles with ornamentation, two or more bulbs, or a bamboo shape had to be lathe-turned; and, therefore, date from about 1800 or later. In the late chairs with long straight spindles, the spindles always are much heavier because of lathe-turning, and usually fewer in number.

In my research on Windsors, I discovered something I hadn't been aware of before. The earliest Windsors, which took the place of late Jacobean and Pilgrim chairs, were eighteen inches from the floor to the top of the front of the seat. This measurement corresponds to that of the chairs they replaced. The height gradually was lowered to about seventeen, then to sixteen inches. So, all of those chairs with fifteen inch seats most likely were cut down for one reason or another. Natural wear may account for about one-quarter to one-half inch from the bottoms of the legs. Because they were of maple they didn't wear down much. Occasionally, you may find an honestly low Windsor; but, unfortunately, many have been cut down. There should be about four-and-a-half to five inches between the side stretchers and the floor if the chair hasn't been lowered. *Slipper* chairs do exist, but not in the numbers we now find for sale, and not very often in the Windsor style.

An early Windsor with original rockers would be an extremely rare item. Most Windsors made before 1800, which have rockers, are wrong. I'm sure there are exceptions; but, most of us will never own one. If you see a Windsor rocker with no side stretchers, and no evidence that there ever were any, you are looking at an original, but late, chair.

Since many of the earliest Windsors often were made to order, a standard size for the seats doesn't seem to exist. However, most seats of the early side chairs had a width of sixteen or seventeen inches, while some armchairs had seats as wide as twenty-five inches. The depth of the seats may run from fifteen to twenty-one inches; but, in most cases, the seats were about two inches thick.

In early bow or braced-back Windsors, the bows usually had two fine grooves cut into the front surface, one near each edge. The back of the bow should be nicely rounded. Reproductions generally have a heavier bow with grooves which are too wide. The bow in the early chairs passes through the seat and is wedged on the underside, while on some reproductions, it doesn't go completely through. The spindles of an early bowback should not pass all the way through the seat; but, the center three or four may go through the bow and be wedged, as may the bracing spindles in a brace-back. If the spindles go through the seat, something is wrong. Maybe they have been replaced.

On these Windsors, the legs usually went through the seat and were wedged; sometimes, however, they did not pass completely through. Both are correct; and, either may be found. However, in most late, factory-made pieces, the legs do not go through. The stretchers should not pass through the legs. If they do, one or more of the following has happened: there has been some bad restoration; or, someone has overscraped and sanded the leg which might reveal the end of a stretcher; or, the stretcher itself may have been replaced.

With Windsor armchairs, look for breaks, especially on the one-piece bow and arm or continuous arm. Where the bow becomes the arm is a very weak point; check it carefully. On a bowback chair with arms, look at where the arms are attached, which also is a very weak joint and often has been cracked or repaired. In addition, check the top of the bow where the spindles go into it. There sometimes is a break just behind the hole, another very weak spot.

Damage to any of these areas is hard to repair and may be very expensive to have fixed. Also, check every spindle, top and bottom, for breaks. And, when examining any Windsor, check the seat to make sure it has not split from drying. Look at the legs to see if they have been cracked or broken where they enter the seat. Finally, if the chair is a "little loose", it will have to be totally reglued and wedged to make it usable. So keep all of this in mind when you are planning to buy.

Be sure the stretchers, spindles, and legs all agree in style. There are a lot of Windsors for sale today which have been made up from several different broken chairs. This is called a *marriage*, and, in many cases, works out pretty well. A married piece may be a fine buy and suit your needs. But, you really should know what you are getting and pay accordingly.

Beware of new paint, especially if it is pretty thick. It is probably covering a multitude of sins such as holes filled with filler, new pieces, bad repairs, etc. If the paint appears to be very old or original and you are paying a high price, be sure it is. Check the underside of the chair seat for any evidence of another color under the present one.

The earliest Windsors often were an Indian red which apparently was more of a stain than a paint. Dark green seems to have been the most used color. This may be over the red stain; also, red paint may be found, again sometimes over the red stain. Yellow was used occasionally, but usually on youth chairs. Brown also may be found as an original color. But, this is rare. If the chair is black, the paint is probably hiding something. If the color is "ping-pong table" green, it most certainly is not original! And if the color is white, just remember how hard it will be to remove every trace of the paint. Windsors after 1800 may be any number of colors; some Sheraton bamboo-styles even were painted to look like bamboo!

Occasionally, you will find a signed Windsor. Before you pay a premium because of this, be sure the name is authentic and is that of a known Windsor chairmaker of an early period. Contemporary chairmakers sign their chairs too! If the name is applied with a modern pencil or new-looking paint, be careful. Most of the signed chairs have the name branded or cut into the underside of the seat. And, occasionally, you may find a label on the bottom of the seat. But, be sure the label belongs to that chair and is honestly old.

Generally, you can tell the origin of an early Windsor by the style of its legs. The straight taper below the bulbous turning is a New England feature. The exception to this is the Rhode Island leg where the taper curves. In contrast, the chairs made in the Pennsylvania and New Jersey area either have a ball at the end of the leg or terminate in the blunt arrow style. I'm sure there are exceptions. But, this information seems to be the general rule.

There are a lot of Windsor chairs for sale in antiques shops and at shows in a very wide range of prices and conditions. Only a few are early, pre-Revolutionary. Quite a few were made during the middle period, from the 1770s to about 1800. And, there are a lot that have been made since then which have experienced a great deal of use. These are the ones you must learn to identify and either stay away from or buy as inexpensively as possible, knowing what they are.

SLAT-BACK CHAIRS

Slat-back and *ladder-back* chairs often are considered one and the same; although slat-backs do indeed have *ladders* suspended by two end posts, here the phrase *ladder-back* is reserved for the Chippendale chairs and settees which also have ladders supported by vertical end posts. So, I'm refering to slat-back chairs, not ladder-backs.

Slat-backs have been made in America since the Pilgrim period. They still are being made, some in factories in the South and some by fine chairmakers. These craftsmen may have woodworking shops

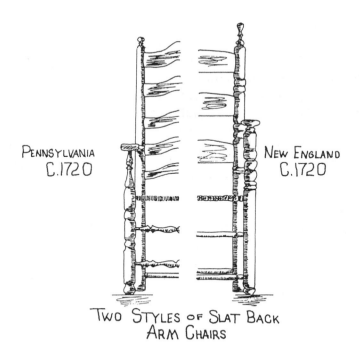

PENNSYLVANIA   NEW ENGLAND
C.1720   C.1720

TWO STYLES OF SLAT BACK
ARM CHAIRS

any place. Most of the 20th century factory-made chairs are easy to spot; usually they are made of oak or ash and have either a fiber rush or an imitation splint seat; in both cases, the seat material is heavy paper. The chairs usually are bulky, have non-descript, if any, finials, and generally are of poor design. But, they are great chairs for children, for a busy family kitchen or den, or for people who just can't take it easy on slat-backs. Whether stained or painted, these chairs are quite practical; but remember, they're not antiques; and, you shouldn't pay a lot for them.

Slat-back chairs can be found in nearly every period of American furniture, from the rather heavy Pilgrim examples to the lightweight, delicate Shaker chairs, and from the bold Pennsylvania slat-back armchairs to the neat sausage-turned New England examples. There are Delaware Valley chairs, English chairs, reproductions, and so on.

One of the nice things about collecting slat-back chairs, other than the fact they are something you can use, is that there are so many different styles to choose from. Your best bet for getting a set of slat-backs is to assemble one yourself. If you find a matching set of early slat-back chairs, they most likely will be rather expensive. If you do find a set which are what you are looking for, you don't have the time to search them out one at a time, and you have the money, buy them. That's a good combination!

If you are going to assemble a set, first decide what period or style you would like. What type of finial do you want? What style of slat? How many slats? What kind of seat, splint or rush? Refinished or painted? If painted, what color? Obviously, there are lots of factors to consider with slat-back chairs, so many, in fact, that you could have either a fun time or a very frustrating time putting together a set! Before you start, you might want to research the market a bit to see which of the styles that appeal to you are more or less available. Some are rather common while others are quite scarce.

I know of folks who have assembled sets of Delaware Valley slat-backs, New England sausage-turned chairs, Shaker slat-backs, and other fairly common styles in a relatively short period of time. However, I also have seen people search for years for a certain type of finial on a six slat chair.

Some people don't worry about whether the finials match, as long as each chair has the same number of slats, while others don't count the slats, as long as the finials look pretty much the same; basically, it is up to the collector—how much time you want to devote, how much money you wish to spend, and how fussy you are about things matching.

Since most of the chairs will be under a table, assuming you are using the set as dining chairs, I would pay more attention to the finials and slats than to the type of seat. If a slat-back is old and has been used a great deal, there is a good chance the seat isn't original. Although replacing a real rush seat may be expensive, it is a relatively minor expense compared to that of a good five or six slat chair which matches a couple of other chairs you already have.

If you aren't too fussy, you may decide to match the finials and the slats, but not worry about the stretchers. Some early slat-backs have a bold front stretcher; some have two nicely turned front stretchers; and, some chairs have front stretchers which are no different from the side and rear ones. The most expensive and most difficult to find are the nice bold front turnings.

Other than out and out fakes, there is some reworking done to these chairs. A couple of things which often are done, and are worth watching for, are replaced finials and reworked slats. It is fairly easy for a woodworker with a lathe to replace common, ordinary finials with exciting, much sought-after ones. Also, a person with simple woodworking tools can change a plain slat into something like a Delaware Valley design. Be sure to check where the finial joins the top of the end post, especially if the chair is painted. If the end post is out of round, which it should be due to age shrinkage, then the finial also should be. Look for an air gap between the finial and the post. If the chair is unpainted, the grain and color of the finial should match that of the end post it is on.

Reshaping slats doesn't happen a lot; but, it is something to watch for. It is fairly easy to do. Reshaped slats can change the feeling of a chair, therefore changing the price. To check for this, first look at the underside of the slats for evidence of fresh tool marks and/or new-looking stain. Also, watch for sharp edges; if the chair is old, then the sharp edges of the slats should have worn down a bit through the years.

Another thing to look for, which can be done but isn't done a lot, is the changing of the front stretcher(s). If a slat-back has two rather plain front stretchers, the chair would be more valuable if it had one "great" front stretcher. By removing the two, plugging their holes, drilling new holes, and putting in a nice, boldly turned stretcher, the price of the chair goes up. It would be hard to do this if the chair was unpainted; however, if there is a lot of heavy paint on the legs, it might be difficult to detect what was done. Be sure the stretcher has the proper wear and has the same feel and patina as the rest of the chair.

Still another, even more difficult, rework is the changing of the front feet. Again, a good woodworker with a lathe and the desire to cheat can totally change the appearance and value of a chair. As with the finials, look for air gaps; and, if unpainted, check to be sure the grain of the foot and the leg are the same. If there is a lot of heavy paint, you only can look as closely as possible and hope.

Slat-back armchairs are scarcer than side chairs. Therefore, you can expect to pay more for one. They also are subject to lots or reworking. You not only have to check the finials, slats, and feet, but, in addition, you have to be sure the arms are right. I have seen several otherwise plain chairs with the wrong arms. In all fairness, the arms often were broken, and needed to be replaced. However, many times they are replaced with much more elegant arms than should be there. Whether the arms look right or not, it's a good idea to make sure they are, if you can. Look at the undersides for the wrong type of tool marks, raw wood, or new stain. Generally, it is rather difficult to change a side chair into an armchair. However, it can be done!

Another type of slat-back which I often see mislabelled is the English version. There aren't a lot of them on the market; but, they are there. So, watch for them if you are looking for a set of slat-backs. There are two things about the English chairs which are unlike the American ones. First, the slats. The English version often has a double serpentine cut in the bottom edge of a slat. Also, the front legs usually are unlike any of American design, with a small pad foot at the base of the leg. When you look at one of these slat-backs, you will notice that it has some features from different areas of America. The finial may look a bit New England while the end post may be plain like that on a chair from the Pennsylvania or New Jersey area; and, the front legs seem to resemble New England legs.

All of this on one chair! Often the wood is either cherry or oak. These are nice chairs; but, whether one at a time or in a set, don't pay the price for them that you would for American chairs. Learn to identify the English slat-backs if you are in the market for chairs. It may save you a lot of trouble and money!

Slat-back chairs sometimes seem to be priced "by the slat". It appears that the more slats, the more expensive the chair. Matching pairs or sets of chairs with six slats are very rare and quite expensive. So, if that is what you want, be prepared. One exception to this may be some of the dining chairs from various Shaker communities. Some of these chairs have very low backs so that they can be slid under the table. Sometimes, they have only one slat, maybe two. These chairs would command a high price, and probably a higher price than non-Shaker, four-slat chairs. However, be careful!

Nothing is sacred. I once pointed out to a show manager that one of his exhibitors had a "pair of Watervliet, New York Shaker dining chairs" for sale which were nothing more than a pair of mid to late 19th century slat-backs which had been cut down, leaving only the bottom two slats. They most likely had been simple three-slat chairs. And, someone reworked them. Whoever did it didn't do a very good job; the ends of the posts showed fresh stain and no wear. The dealer removed the sign, but left a copy of Robert Meader's *Guide to Shaker Furniture* open to the page showing the dining chairs. Fortunately, they didn't sell there; but, I don't know what happened to them.

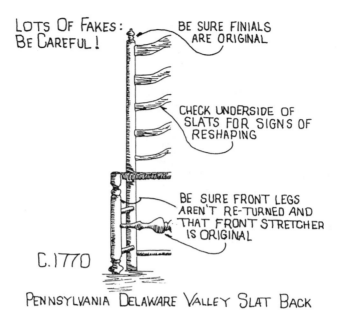

LOTS OF FAKES:
BE CAREFUL!

BE SURE FINIALS
ARE ORIGINAL

CHECK UNDERSIDE OF
SLATS FOR SIGNS OF
RESHAPING

BE SURE FRONT LEGS
AREN'T RE-TURNED AND
THAT FRONT STRETCHER
IS ORIGINAL

C. 1770

PENNSYLVANIA DELAWARE VALLEY SLAT BACK

As with other items of antique furniture, if a type or style becomes scarce or "in", it likely will be copied or faked until the public gets wise, or until something else becomes more popular. This is true with slat-backs; and, since they still are rather popular, it is good to be careful when planing to add this kind of chair to your collection.

PAINTED PLANK SEAT CHAIRS

Painted *plank seat* chairs could be called "fancy chairs", although they aren't what we think of when someone mentions fancy chairs. They also could be called Windsors. But, we have to draw a line here, separating what we generally consider a Windsor chair and what I'm covering as a plank seat chair. The definition of a Windsor chair is, "A wooden chair with spindle back, raking legs, and usually a saddle seat". Some books define Windsors as bent-back wooden seat chairs. Of course, this is fine for early examples. Here, I am going to discuss the plank seat chairs which followed what generally is considered the good Windsors.

I could find some argument in calling the bamboo-styled chairs Windsors, while not referring to the other solid wooden seat chairs of the same period as Windsors; but, that's the way I feel about it.

After the war of 1812, more and more different styles of chairs started to appear on the market. Some of them looked like a combination of late Windsor and fancy chair. Elaborate painting began to replace the plain paint on the preceding chairs. Not only was there a lot of fancy, realistic grain-painting, but also a lot of scenes, flowers, leaves, etc. Instead of the straight, long spindles of earlier Windsors, we have half-spindles, arrow-shaped spindles, both straight and bent, some long spindles but fewer than in earlier chairs, and splats replacing spindles.

Not only is there a large variety of spindles in these chairs, there also is quite an assortment of upper back rails. Unlike the simple bent-back found in an early Windsor, or the bamboo turning found in the Sheraton Windsor, there is the pillow-back, crown-back, variations of the crown-back, roll-top back, slat-top with rabbit ears, sometimes called thumb-back end posts, step-down, and on, and on. As you can see, with the array of spindles and backs, there is quite a variety of plank seat chairs to be found. However, there are some patterns to all of this.

Half-spindle chairs generally have a flat upper rail which is held to the end posts by screws, usually from the rear. These upper rails may be plain or have *angel wing* cut outs on the ends. Often, such chairs were made in Pennsylvania; however, later examples can be found from other areas, particularly New England, the South, and the Midwest.

Half-spindle chairs with pillow-backs almost always are from New England and often were made by the Hitchcock factory or someone trying to copy. The half-spindles themselves may number three, four, or five.

Arrow-back chairs most often have end posts terminating in rabbit ears. However, there are exceptions; some arrow-backs have a slat-top and turned end posts which are round all the way to the top, while others have a flat upper rail similar to the half-spindle type. If the arrow-shaped spindles are bent, the end posts also will be. Generally, this style has a slat-top rail. There may be three or four arrows; four usually indicates an earlier and more desirable chair. Therefore, it generally costs more. Often, this style of chair is from New York or the New England states.

Full length spindles usually end in a slat-top rail which is held in place with round end posts. There may be four or more spindles in one of these chairs. More is most desirable. This style of chair was made in any number of places, from Maine to South Carolina, and from New Jersey to Kansas. Usually they are referred to as Windsors; but, I call them "Windsor-types". These chairs have been made continuously from about 1800.

The main thing to remember when thinking of buying one or a set is to check everything very carefully. Be sure the seat(s) is made from one piece of soft wood, and that the underside of the seat is smoothed with a hand plane. This doesn't prove the chair is old; but, there is a better chance of if being old than a similar piece with a glued-up seat and machine marks on the bottom! This applies to ALL plank seat chairs and benches.

A center splat, balloon-back chair is almost always from Pennsylvania; but, there may be exceptions. This is a general rule. If the seat is made of poplar, you pretty well can count on the chair being from the Keystone state. The Pennsylvania Germans are credited with the design and construction of this style of chair. It is very pretty; but, because of the design, it isn't always the best buy if you plan to use the chair where it will get a lot of use, such as the kitchen. The top rail shrinks in one direction while the two end posts shrink in the opposite direction; this often makes the back loose. Then, you have only two small end posts and a thin center splat holding the weight and pressure of the sitter's back. If the chair is loose due to shrinkage, it is very vulnerable to breakage. These chairs may be considered prettier than a lot of other plank seat chairs from the same period. But, they aren't the strongest. And, therefore, they must be kept in good condition.

Actually, this is true with ALL chairs; "a little loose" is, or can be, very destructive. That is why stretchers break, end posts break off at the seat, and a number of other things happen to your chairs.

Splats in various designs were used in other plank seat chairs, in addition to the balloon-backs. They were used with the flat upper rail and the slat-top rail backs.

Take any one of the aforementioned plank seat chairs, stretch it out, and you have a plank seat bench. The makeup of the back combination is the same with benches as with the chairs. They just were

BOTH TYPES WERE PAINTED— OFTEN GRAINED

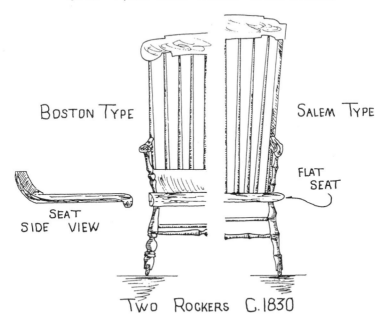

BOSTON TYPE   SALEM TYPE

FLAT
SEAT

SEAT
SIDE VIEW

TWO ROCKERS C.1830

longer. One exception is the combination of splats and full spindles used together in some benches.

An addition to the styles mentioned above is the cradle-rocker or *Mammy's Bench.* Usually, this bench is about long enough for three average-sized people. There are no center legs; and, the end legs have rockers attached to them. There also is a *gate* affair, which is removable, that forms the cradle when in place.

As with the chairs, it often is very difficult to tell just where a bench originated. They were made all through New England, New York, New Jersey, and Pennsylvania at first, then, later, wherever there were woodworkers and the need for plank seat benches. As the population moved west, so did the making of the necessary furnishings.

Another style of chair with fancy paint is the rocker, particularly the *Salem* and the very popular *Boston* rockers. The most obvious difference between these two chairs is that the Salem has a flat seat and isn't as fancy as the Boston. The front legs of the Boston are more elaborate than those of the Salem. Both styles may have either straight or curved end posts and spindles. Needless to say, the curved examples are much more comfortable and, therefore, more expensive, since they are more sought after. The Salem rocker is comfortable; but, one of the most comfortable chairs ever created by the early designers has to be the Boston rocker! With its heavy scrolled seat, nicely curved arms, and gently curving spindles, it "fits" nearly anyone.

In all of my years in the antiques business, I only once heard someone say a Boston rocker was "the most uncomfortable chair I ever sat in". That was several years ago; and, I'm still trying to figure out that comment! In any case for most people, both chairs are very comfortable. Some later, more Empire-looking, Boston rockers have a wide, curved center splat. This style also is rather comfortable; but, aesthetically, it is bulky and cumbersome when compared to the earlier, spindle-back examples.

Most Salem rockers were made in the New England area, as were many Boston rockers. However, a lot of "Boston"-style chairs were made elsewhere. Unless one of these is signed, you must rely on the wood to give you a hint of where it started life. If the seat is made of poplar instead of pine, there is a good chance the chair wasn't made in New England; it probably was made in the Pennsylvania area.

Plank seat chairs, benches, and rockers which are in a "natural" finish have been refinished at some point in time. It would be rather rare to find one of these which had never been painted. The earliest of this group of seating devices were painted either red or black. Then, we find graining, usually of rosewood, walnut, or fancy mahogany. Still later, starting in the Baltimore area, we find yellow. In the Pennsylvania region, there is quite a variety of colors including red, yellow, several greens, black, brown, and combinations. Over this assortment of paint colors and fancy graining, there can be found scenes, flowers, fruit, leaves, striping, gilding, and whatever the artist wanted to do, or whatever he was commissioned to do.

Because so many of the plank seat chairs, benches, and rockers were "refinished" a few years ago (sadly, some still are finding their way to the stripping tanks), a lot of them have been repainted. As has been mentioned here so many times, repainting is all right if you know it, and pay accordingly. Look for paint in cracks, over repairs, over worn areas, and over other places where there shouldn't be paint. Check the underside of the seat, where the legs join, for a different color. Also, look at the underside of the back top rail for new paint over old. If the chair has been repainted, you most likely will see a different color in one of these areas. If the item was "dipped" to remove the paint, these same areas probably will show an off color of wood, sort of oxidized. This oxidized wood is most obvious on the underside of the seat.

If you keep searching and are lucky, you may find a chair or bench which was signed by the person who painted it. Often the painter was proud of his work and felt that a little advertising couldn't hurt! If you do find a name which is in paint, the color should be the same as is found in the decoration somewhere. On the other hand, the furniture maker, if he signed the piece, often used chalk or a branding iron, leaving his imprint in the underside of the seat. In the case of makers such as Hitchcock, whose workers both made and painted the items, the name usually is stencilled someplace such as on the rear of the seat or on the back of the top rail.

Sets of plank seat chairs with original paint now are getting rather expensive. However, they are not nearly as costly as a matching set of good Windsors; so, you may want to look for these comfortable chairs for your diningroom.

If you aren't in a big hurry, you could spend some time searching out a set of plank seat chairs, one or two at a time. Buy a pair; take photographs of them; then, set out to find chairs that match, until you have the size set you want. If you do it this way, be sure the first ones you buy are not repainted, and that they have a design you will be able to locate. Don't buy a pair which were made and painted in Maine, then try to match them at shops and shows in Ohio! This could be very frustrating. Try to locate something which will be relatively easy to find in other shops in the major area of your antiquing. Putting together a set this way usually is less expensive and can be a lot of fun!

FANCY CHAIRS

When I say *fancy* chair, most people think of either a Hitchcock or Hitchcock-type chair or of a Sheraton style chair. Both are fancy chairs. There were several makers of fancy chairs in the early 1800s, up until about the mid-1800s when Lambert Hitchcock died and Victorian furnishings came into vogue. Hitchcock should get the recognition for spreading the style with his prolific production of chairs, especially in the early years of this period. Although Henry Ford gets a lot of credit, Lambert Hitchcock really was one of the first to make the most of mass production.

Fancy chairs were popular during the Federal and American Empire periods, which were the years between about 1780 and 1850. Around 1850, the Victorian period was becoming established. These years covered the end of the Chippendale period and all of the Adam, Hepplewhite, Sheraton, and Empire periods. This also is the time during which Duncan Phyfe did his work; therefore, it also can be called the Phyfe period.

Fancy chairs generally were that—fancy. They were light in appearance and weight and were very pretty, with none of the heaviness of most of the earlier styles. There really aren't any "country" or "primitive" fancy chairs, although those made of maple, birch, pine, or poplar, which then were painted to look like better woods such as mahogany, rosewood, or walnut, do fit in with most country settings, if done carefully. More about this type a bit later; first, let's cover the beginnings of the fancy chair.

Although the Federal period started with the Revolution, the furniture styles of the period still were greatly influenced by England; Adam, Hepplewhite, and Sheraton, all Englishmen, were copied over and over throughout this period. These styles and designs either were made and sold in England, made in England and sold in America, or made and sold in America.

Adam, the earliest of the three main designers, had a lot of the Chippendale influence in his earliest chairs; then, he slowly moved away from these influences into his own designs, with heavy wheel-looking backs and more reeding of the legs. Overlapping the Adam school of design came the designs of George Hepplewhite. Here we see a more graceful chair, with backs in a shield shape, as well as oval and a few hoop shapes. The legs were lighter than those on chairs by Adam, and generally tapered; at times, they ended in spade feet.

During the early Hepplewhite period, Thomas Sheraton started to make his mark in the furniture design world. While most of the Hepplewhite chair backs were curved, most of Sheraton's were straight lines, usually square or rectangular, especially in the early years. This is one of the easiest ways to tell these two styles apart. With Sheraton, we really started getting into true fancy chairs, which continued through the American Empire and early Victorian periods.

The fancy chairmakers copied one another a great deal. It would appear the workers went from chairmaker to chairmaker, taking

BALTIMORE STYLE   NEW YORK STYLE

TWO "FANCY" CHAIRS   C. 1810

their talents and certain styles with them. It is very hard to tell one from another; in some cases, even the painting is the same. Most fancy chairs are painted, sometimes with gold leaf decoration. This is particularly true with chairs from New England and New York.

The chairs made in the Baltimore area tended to be a bit more formal in feeling than the ones made further north. White and yellow were used a great deal as base colors in these Southern examples. With the "squareness" of the early Sheraton styles, the backs offered a nice flat area on which to paint a scene or an important building. This also was done with some of the fancy chairs made elsewhere, but was quite popular in the South on early examples.

Most fancy chairs had either cane or rush seats, helping to make them rather light, both in weight and appearance. Also, there are some plank-seat chairs painted this way; however, they usually are referred to as plank-seat chairs, not fancy chairs. But, they were produced during this same period.

Many of the fancy chairs made during this time are called *Hitchcocks*; however, there were many makers. Unless you can see a name on the chair, it could have been made by any number of different chairmakers. Makers names usually were stencilled on the rear of the seat. If the chair had a cane seat, the frame was solid; if the seat was rush, there usually was a thin strip of wood covering the edge of the seat which is where the name would be. Some makers stencilled their name on the lower edge of the back of the top slat. On some

Boston-type rockers, the name could be along the upper front edge of the rear of the seat.

Fancy chairs were made along the East Coast from Baltimore to Boston, including New York City and Philadelphia. Toward the late 1800s, they were made inland from the Carolinas to Chicago. I would guess that the largest number of fancy chairs were made in New York City or Connecticut. Both areas turned out great quantities of these very popular items for the middle class of that time.

Since chairs generally get so much use, you would expect a lot of the original paint on a fancy chair to have been rubbed off through the years. Many of these chairs have been repainted. Unfortunately, a large number were "refinished", by or for someone who either didn't like paint or couldn't put up with worn and chipping paint, and couldn't find anyone to re-paint them properly.

Collectors of antique furniture go through phases; there will be a time when they are looking for painted furniture. Then, there will be a period when they want everything refinished. This last phase has done a great deal of damage to a good many early pieces of painted furniture. Several years ago, 25 to 40, many collectors wanted things pretty, refinished; during that era, a sad number of fancy chairs were refinished. Generally this was before the proliferation of so many "dip-and-strip" places; so, these chairs were scraped to their raw wood, sometimes stained, and finished "natural". I am the first to admit that in the late 1950s I was one of the refinishers who was doing this terrible thing. All of a sudden, I realized what I was doing to history, and refused to refinish anything which had good, original paint. Now, I am one of those who tries to restore and save original paints and finishes.

In any case, because of such times, there are a large number of fancy chairs which are either in unpainted condition or repainted. The unpainted are obvious; it's the repainted ones you must watch for. As I have mentioned several times on these pages, a repainted piece is all right, as long as you know and pay accordingly. Most people would rather live with a nicely repainted piece of furniture than a piece with flaking, chipping paint; just be aware that a repainted piece isn't worth as much as an untouched one.

If a chair has been repainted by a professional who knows how to grain, gild, etc., and who has followed an original design, it may be very difficult, if not nearly impossible, to tell that it was done, unless the paint looks or smells fresh. One thing to watch for is paint over worn areas; there shouldn't be any; after all, if the edge of the seat is very worn, or a stretcher has had a lot of shoes rubbing it through the years, the paint would be the first thing to wear away!

Whether the chair has a rush or cane seat, check the seat material for paint. Look next to any painted areas. Usually, the original chairs were painted before the seat was put in. Sometimes, the seat of a fancy chair may have been painted; this was done to help preserve the seat, to help make it last longer, but isn't likely to be original.

Since fancy chairs still are being made today, the Hitchcock Chair Company in Riverton, Connecticut is one of the makers, and there are others, you would be wise to know the difference between the new and the old. Generally, the new chairs are heavier in look and feel. It would be good if you could find a furniture outlet which sells the new ones to look at some of them. Then, go to a museum or house restoration and check out a truly old, original, chair. That's the best way to get a feel for the difference. Once you really see these differences, you'll have no problem telling the chairs apart.

Another thing to watch for is replaced parts; since these chairs are rather light, they are somewhat fragile. Often, one has a replaced leg, stretcher, or back piece. Again, a good repair is all right; a bad one is an eye-sore; but, both should be pointed out. And, you should pay accordingly.

One more thing: there were some fancy chairs made of tiger and/or bird's eye maple which never were painted; they are few and far between, but well worth the search, if you collect this type of maple furniture.

Many of these chairs are painted to look like walnut or rosewood with only a small amount of gilding and stencilling on them. They are fine dining chairs; but, after dinner you will want to move to something more comfortable; this move will help prevent "non-thinkers" from tilting back in these light chairs!

ROCKING CHAIRS

At one time or another, both Benjamin Franklin and the Shakers have been given credit for inventing the rocker, for converting straight chairs into rocking chairs. Both credits are wrong! Franklin was born in 1706; the Shakers didn't even get here until 1774; and, there is evidence that rockers were in use, albeit limited, before Ben was born.

As Americans, we can be proud that the rocking chair seems to have started here. There isn't any information indicating that they were made in England or Europe until after they were in use here. In my research, the earliest examples of rocking chairs seem to have come from coastal New England sometime after 1650, but before 1700; that's pretty early for this style of chair. Rockers were used on cradles, in England, Europe, and here, long before then; but, for some reason, apparently, they never were adapted to chairs until around this time.

Franklin, being a person who reportedly enjoyed creature comforts, may have designed and/or contracted for the making of rocking chairs for himself and others in his area; but he couldn't have invented them. A few slat-back chairs and some Windsors, both of which are from his period in time, have rockers. He may have had something to do with their manufacture; it is hard to determine. And, I'm sure he did design some of them.

Rockers were not applied to, or designed for use on, "classy" styles. Rocking chairs were available during the Queen Anne and Chippendale periods; but, you don't see any rockers on chairs of either style, unless they were added at a later date. Rocking chairs, like Windsors, were not used in the parlors; instead, they were degraded to the kitchen, bedroom, extra rooms, or the servants' quarters; neither type of chair held the status it does today. Because of this, proof of early inventories showing "chairs with rockers" are very unusual. There are a few exceptions.

Through the 1700s, rocking chairs became more and more popular; and, by 1800, lots of these comfortable chairs could be found. Even earlier style chairs were being converted, especially Windsors and slat-backs. Also, many slat-back chairs were made with rockers; wherever these chairs were being produced, in New England, the mid-Atlantic, the South, and, later, in the Midwest, there were some with rockers being made.

By 1800, the Shakers were producing chairs, and continued to make rocking chairs in one style or another until the late 1800s. The Shakers may not have invented them; but they are believed to be the first to more or less mass-produce rocking chairs, after designing simple styles and then the equipment to manufacture them rapidly.

By 1810 to 1820, there were Sheraton chairs with rockers, and after that, some Empire-style rocking chairs. The styles from these two periods are about as "fancy" as rocking chairs ever got.

Boston, Salem, and Hitchcock rockers were soon to follow, being made by about 1825 or so; and, I might add, a form of these three chairs has been made ever since, up to today.

Since rocking chairs are rather popular, I'm going to devote some time telling you how to determine if the rockers are original, because a great many aren't.

First of all, if you see a Boston, Salem, or large Hitchcock rocking chair, it is not a conversion; the only thing to watch for here is whether or not the rockers have been replaced. They often are. The rockers on most of these were rather thin and not too sturdy which led to frequent breakage. Look closely for repairs or replacement. Check the fit, and the color of the paint; or, if the chair is refinished, look for evidence that the rockers are original. It's all right if the rockers are properly repaired or replaced, as long as you know, and pay accordingly.

Most of the Shaker rocking chairs you encounter will not be conversions either. There were so many rockers made, converting a chair usually wasn't necessary. However, if you are in the market for a Shaker rocking chair, be sure it is Shaker! There are a lot of chairs, as well as other pieces of furniture, called Shaker which aren't. If you want to be sure, visit a museum or check any one of several good reference books on Shaker furniture. Nearly every piece of Shaker furniture and most of their designs can be found in books, unlike many primitive and country pieces which often are one-of-a-kind items.

On many of the late Shaker chairs, made after the Civil War, you may find a decal. On the rocking chairs, it usually was applied to a rocker; if you see this, you can be fairly sure the rocker is not a replacement. If, however, someone refinished the chair, chances are good that the decal was removed with the original finish, devaluing the chair and removing the "proof" of its authenticity. By the mid-1870s, nearly all of the Shaker chairs had decals. It's the earlier ones you must be careful of. The chairs made from the late 1700s to the mid-1800s outside of the Shaker communities but in the same areas often looked a lot like those being turned out by the Shakers. Without comparing one of these with an authentic chair, you might be convinced it is Shaker, pay a high price, and be very wrong. A lot of plain, simple, New England and New York pieces are passed off as Shaker; be careful!

If you see a Windsor with rockers, how do you know whether they are original or replacements? A great deal is guesswork; however,

ROCKERS MOST LIKELY NOT ORIGINAL BECAUSE OF
THE STRETCHER LOCATION – CHECK CLOSELY!

there are things to watch for. First of all, early Windsors did not have rockers; so, if the chair you are looking at is early, with an *H* stretcher, there is a good chance the rockers are a later addition. Around 1800, there were some Windsors made with rockers. If the chair has an H stretcher, the ends of the legs should be a bit heavy so they could be cut out to accommodate rockers. If you are looking at a bamboo turned Sheraton Windsor, ca. 1810–1820, with rockers, you will note that the side stretchers either are missing or are higher than usual, if the rockers are original. If there is a stretcher and it is too close to the rocker to look right, then you most likely have a conversion. Windsor rocking chairs, both with H stretchers and box stretchers, are not too common; so, when you look at one, be careful. All of the comments I've made on previous pages about wood color, paint color, patina, etc. apply here.

I guess the type of chair most often converted to a rocker is the slat-back. There were many of these chairs made as rockers; but, most likely, more have been converted. This is not to say that all of the slat-back rockers you'll see are conversions. But, it is wise to be very careful.

When examining a slat-back rocking chair, be aware of the following: Look for evidence of a stretcher, about where the rocker is connected to the leg; or, if the bottom stretcher is still there, it shouldn't be close to the rocker. If the chair was made for rockers, the stretchers were aesthetically correct, pleasing to the eye. Often, the bottoms of the legs were swelled out a bit to accept the cut-outs for the rockers. You may find both New England and Pennsylvania styled slat-backs with rockers, some original, some conversions. They usually are armchairs.

In most cases, the earlier the rocking chair, the shorter the rockers. There rarely is much of an extension in the front of the chair; but, the later the chair, the longer the rocker protrudes in the rear. After a few years of folks going over backwards in chairs with short rockers, the evolution process worked, and the rockers slowly became longer! Some restorers, who may attempt to fool some of the people some of the time, know this; and, they may shorten a long rocker to give a later chair an earlier look. Always examine the bottom and rear end of a short rocker, to see if it had been longer at some point. This may not be done a lot; but, it is something to know about and watch for.

I feel it is fairly safe to say that nearly all but Empire rocking chairs were painted when they were newly made. Since most of them are simple country designs, you wouldn't expect anything else. Some of the Shaker chairs were not painted or stained, especially the early ones. But, most of the later ones, which we are likely to see for sale, were. As for Windsor, Sheraton, slat-back, and plank-seat chairs, they were painted, as were the Boston, Salem, and Hitchcock rockers. The Empire examples generally were not painted, but finished "natural", showing the pretty wood they were made of. However, these chairs are not common.

If you are looking for a rocking chair, and you want one in paint, try to find one in original paint. A repainted chair may be hiding a lot of repairs; if it is supposed to be original paint, be sure it is. Look for a different color under the "original", and watch for paint over wear areas and cracks in the wood. If the chair is refinished, you should be able to spot any repaired or replaced pieces.

A note about the Boston rocker here—although they were painted and decorated, these chairs usually had their arms finished natural, since the arms almost always were made of walnut, mahogany, or cherry.

Nearly any room has a good spot for a rocking chair. They not only are good looking, but also generally are very comfortable. There are few things more relaxing than sitting in a rocking chair, as long as it "fits" you. I find some are too large for me, or the seat too deep. However, once one fits, it is a delightful way to spend some "thinking" time!

BEDSTEADS OR BEDS

What we refer to as a bed really is a *bedstead;* the bedding itself is the bed. In my research for this book, I found that the framework, usually made of wood, should be referred to as a bedstead; all of the paraphernalia that goes under and over you while you are lying down is called the bed.

From earliest times, the bedstead always has been very important. Ancient drawings show well-developed beds in Egypt, Rome, Greece, Persia, etc. Some of the early structures were made of wood, others metal or rock. Then, they were covered with animal skins and/or textiles for comfort and warmth. From these early times to the present, bedsteads have gone through many style changes, yet have remained basically the same; their purpose hasn't changed; so, you wouldn't expect them to have undergone many drastic changes. They have gone from skin-covered stone, to cloth-draped "room-within-a-room" around the 12th century, to some of the "water-beds" of today. I'm not going to get into skin-covered stone or plastic-covered waterbeds. Here, we just will discuss the bedsteads made and used from the 17th to 19th centuries.

Let's start with the bedsteads with high posts. They were and are called by any of these names; *canopy, high post,* and *tester.* Tester can be pronounced either tēster or tester, according to my dictionary. That word came into the English language during the 14th century. High posts made very thin, usually of rural origin often are referred to as *pencil posts.*

The early high post bedsteads were either for privacy or warmth, depending upon the part of the country in which they were used. As houses became larger, people had extra money to have more fireplaces built. Later, stoves or other sources of heat appeared. Because of this, the original purpose of the canopy no longer was valid. But, styles are slow to change. So, the wealthy, who could afford the elegant bedding and canopies when they were necessary, kept them in vogue when they were only for style or decoration. There hardly are any bedsteads before the Chippendale period with nice woodwork. Because of all of the draping of material, you couldn't see the woodwork.

By the late 18th century, the canopy still was being used, as was the head draping. Since this material covered the head posts, they were simple and often of a plain wood, while the foot posts were nicely turned and/or carved, and usually were made of a good hardwood, often mahogany. This practice carried over into the Sheraton period, but soon gave way to all of the posts being of the same style. Usually, they were nicely done of a hardwood. The fabric slowly disappeared until it covered only the tester or canopy of the bedstead. At this time, the headboard became more important and, therefore, more decorative. This style has persisted in one way or another, and still is found on reproduction bedsteads in furniture stores.

While all of this was going on in the wealthier homes, the poor, the hired, and the children slept in much different bedsteads. There were many low post beds made and used in the early days of this young country. Usually, they were of local hardwoods, and the earliest had either square or octagonal posts, often with the head posts being a bit higher than the foot, and supporting a simple headboard. These early beds almost always were painted a plain color. Starting in the 18th century, simple turned posts began appearing on these low post bedsteads. Usually, these also were painted, often with a plain color. However, sometimes they were painted to look like a more expensive wood, such as mahogany. With these bedsteads, both the posts and the headboard were grained. Sometimes, the rails also were grain-painted. However, usually, they were painted with a plain color.

Both the high post and low post bedsteads were made of local hardwoods, except for the few made of imported mahogany. New England and New York posts usually were of maple or birch, sometimes beech, while the headboards mostly were pine. Bedsteads in the New Jersey and Pennsylvania areas often were maple, and sometimes walnut or cherry, with poplar headboards. This same wood combination also was used in the Southeast where walnut was abundant.

A hired man's bedstead was as simple as possible; basically, it was four low posts with ropes strung between four rails which were held up by the posts to keep the bedding off the floor.

The *trundle bed*, also know as the *truckle bed*, was kept under an adult bedstead and pulled out at night for a child, or, in some cases, for children. These bedsteads often had wheels, which, of course, made them easier to pull out from under the large bedsteads. The

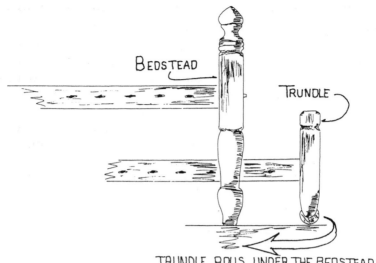

TRUNDLE ROLLS UNDER THE BEDSTEAD

wheels, at times, were parallel to the long (side) rails so that the trundle could be pulled out from the foot of the large bedstead. Some wheels, however, were set into the post so that they were perpendicular to the side rails; this type of trundle could be pulled out from either side. The ones which came out from the side had posts of equal length. But, some of the trundle bedsteads which were pulled out at the foot had two longer head posts, usually with a headboard. These were too high to fit completely under the large unit. When the rest of the trundle was pushed into place, its headboard became sort of a footboard for the larger bedstead.

Some trundle bedsteads were made at the same time as the larger ones and, therefore, are of the same style, wood, and color. To locate one of these sets would be a real find in the antiques market; but, I have seen them.

By the end of the first quarter of the 19th century, there weren't many finely turned high post bedsteads being made. The heavy empire style started to take over, and, with that, came such things as *sleigh beds*. Also, at the same time as sleigh beds, there still were high and low post bedsteads being made. However, they were much heavier than the Sheraton styles, and often had a lot of elaborate carving. They also usually had large, fancy headboards. This heaviness carried over to the Victorian period and persisted for many years. But, with mass production and scarcity of wood, bedsteads, as well as other pieces of furniture, started to look a bit lighter by the end of the 19th century.

Around 1850 or so, the turned or spool bedsteads started appearing. Most of these pieces didn't have solid head or footboards, but were very airy with spindles taking the place of solid wood. Lots of these bedsteads were made for several years. However, since they were so lightly constructed, many have not made it to the late 20th century. There are several to be found today, but not as many as we would expect. Generally, they were made either of walnut or maple stained to look like walnut.

Some bedsteads of this period and style didn't have square rails with pegs for the ropes. Instead, the makers devised a clever way of holding the foot and head sections together with round rails. These rails had threads cut into each end; one end had left-handed threads, the other right-handed. When assembling, you fit the rail between the head and foot posts at the same time and turn; this draws the two ends toward each other. When everything is right, the rail stops with the rope pegs in the up position. Then, when the ropes are put into place, the pressure keeps the rails tight. Very clever at the time! But, through the years, the threads wore, shrunk, and broke; and, often, these bedsteads are difficult to keep together today.

By this time, brass and iron bedsteads were starting to show up and were the "latest" things to have. By 1900, metal springs were very popular and could be bought by anyone with money who wanted them. There still were wooden bedsteads being made at this time; but, most now had metal rails to support the "new" metal springs.

In the early years of the period I'm talking about, there were folding bedsteads; not a lot; but, they were made. Usually, they were folded up in the morning to be out of the way, and were ideal for small homes where space was at a premium. Some of them folded up into a closet or press, and are called *press beds*.

At one time, early in this period, there were other press beds. In this case, the bedstead actually was built into a closet, with both drapes and doors to close off the "press" from the rest of the room. I believe these usually were made in New England.

The type of field or camp bedstead we usually think of is the small portable, folding unit. Usually it doesn't come apart; but, because of its lightness, it is easy to move about.

Bedsteads and bedding generally were very highly prized and often were quite valuable, being one of the top items listed in early estates and inventories. Also, good bedsteads were, and are, very sought after.

When looking for an antique bedstead today, there are several things you should keep in mind. First of all, what do you want? A perfect, untouched example? Or, one that is usable with today's standards? Most untouched bedsteads are too short; some are only 70 inches long, while many are no more than 72 inches. If you find one which is untouched, and you like it, buy it and have new side rails made for it which are 76 inches long. Keep the old rails. DO NOT HAVE THE OLD ONES LENGTHENED. This way, you have kept the original and still made the bedstead usable. And, if you decide later to sell it, you have all of the original pieces.

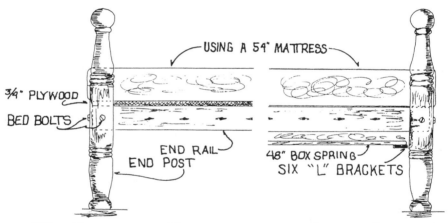

TWO METHODS OF FITTING BEDDING TO ANTIQUE BEDSTEADS

With the rails the right length, the width is easy to work around. There are a couple of ways of handling this. One way is that if the width between the side rails is 48 inches, which it often is, you can fit a three-quarter box spring in there. If you have new side rails made, the person making them can move them out a bit to give you a little extra width. Fasten iron "L" brackets to the new side rails to support the box spring. It should sit in such a way so the mattress will rest just above the side rails. This way, you gain a few inches and most likely can use a full-size mattress on the otherwise too narrow bedstead. Another way to approach the size dilemma is to have someone fit ¾ inch plywood between the side rails in such a way to support a full-size mattress. If you have had the side rails replaced, the plywood can be screwed to the new ones.

If you have decided to leave your untouched bedstead alone and have a mattress custom-made, you can fit ¾ inch plywood between the rope pegs. The pegs will hold the plywood in place so that it won't slip; a slip could allow the occupant to fall to the floor in the middle of the night! You also can rope the bedstead and put a mattress right on the ropes.

If you are looking for a high post bedstead and find just the four posts, you might consider yourself lucky. With these posts, a good woodworker can make your new/old bed to fit any size mattress you want to use, including king. Since everything except the posts already was missing, you don't have to worry about changing anything. A bedstead such as this may not be as valuable as a pure, untouched one; but, it is a lot more practical for today's lifestyles.

A natural piece of furniture to go with a full-size bedstead is a crib and/or cradle. Both are hard to come by in early styles. Most cribs found today are from the Victorian period or later. Most cradles date from the late 1700s through the Victorian period. But, remember, when looking at a cradle, it gets in the way. If you have a baby coming or have a newborn, a cradle is great. However, a child outgrows one rather quickly. And, there's really nothing else you can do with a cradle. So, unless you have plenty of room, I would think twice about buying a crib or cradle.

Bedsteads, whether high post, low post, trundle, or cradle, can be found today in untouched condition, very rough, painted, and in natural finishes. They also are in nearly every price range from a few hundred to many thousands of dollars. With this in mind, if you are bedstead hunting, first, figure out what you want. Then, start looking. Be careful of reworked and repainted, as well as refinished, bedsteads. Untouched, and in original condition, usually are the most expensive. However, a bedstead which suits your needs may be the best buy in the end. This is especially true if you aren't a dealer, and you're buying a bedstead to use for the next several years.

One word of caution, if a modern box spring and mattress fit within the frame of a bedstead, you probably are looking at a reproduction or reworked bedstead. There is nothing wrong with this; just be sure to pay accordingly.

EPILOGUE

Throughout this section on terminology, I have pointed out the importance of knowledge; *YOU CAN'T KNOW TOO MUCH ABOUT A SUBJECT!* And, you can't use the knowledge properly unless you can remember it almost unconsciously. So, you have seen the phrase "Again, take an expert with you" many times in these pages and many more times the words "be careful". In addition, I could list a small library which may be helpful in your search for information. But, that wouldn't help. What you must do as a collector, whether new or advanced, is search through book stores and contact book dealers; there are some who specialize in books on antiques and collectibles. Find a publication which has information on the subject in which you are interested. Ask questions; the folks who sell these books may be able to save you a lot of time if you ask them whether they have anything covering that subject. Ask other collectors and friendly dealers what books they rely on for knowledge. And, above all, don't take everything that you get from one book as the ONLY information. You would be surprised how many times different books give you different bits of information on the same subject. Also, don't forget your local library, museums, and house restorations as sources of knowledge, and, of course, other collectors, many of whom may help you avoid some of the mistakes they have made through the years.

I hope my years of research and experience, some of which I have put on these pages, will help you. It is my wish that what you have read here will help prevent you from making an expensive mistake while giving you the confidence you need to look, learn, and enjoy living with those wonderful, dusty, warm, old pieces of furniture we lovingly call antiques.

Bibliography

Andrews, Edward Deming. THE PEOPLE CALLED SHAKERS. New York: Oxford University Press. 1953

────── and Andrews, Faith. SHAKER FURNITURE: THE CRAFTSMANSHIP OF AN AMERICAN COMMUNAL SECT. Connecticut: Dover Publications, Inc. 1950

──────. RELIGION IN WOOD—A BOOK OF SHAKER FURNITURE. Indiana University Press. 1966

Comstock, Helen. AMERICAN FURNITURE: SEVENTEENTH, EIGHTEENTH, AND NINETEENTH CENTURY STYLES. New York: The Viking Press. 1962

Fairbanks, Jonathan L. and Bates, Elizabeth Bidwell. AMERICAN FURNITURE: 1620 TO THE PRESENT. New York: Richard Marek Publishers. 1981

Fales, Dean A. Jr. AMERICAN PAINTED FURNITURE: 1660–1880. New York: E.P. Dutton and Co., Inc. 1972

──────. THE FURNITURE OF HISTORIC DEERFIELD. New York: E.P. Dutton and Co., Inc. 1976.

Grant, Jerry V. and Allen, Douglas R. SHAKER FURNITURE MAKERS. New Hampshire: University Press of New England. 1989

Hageman, Jane Sikes. OHIO FURNITURE MAKERS: 1790 TO 1845, Vol. One. Ohio: Ohio Furniture Makers. 1989

Janzen, Reinhild Kauenhoven and Janzen, John M. MENNONITE FURNITURE: A MIGRANT TRADITION (1766–1910). Pennsylvania: Good Books. 1991

Johansson, Warren I. COUNTRY FURNITURE AND ACCESSORIES FROM QUEBEC. Pennsylvania: Schiffer Publishing, Ltd. 1990

Joy, E.T. ENGLISH FURNITURE. New York: Arco Publishing Co., Inc. 1962

Kauffman, Henry. PENNSYLVANIA DUTCH: AMERICAN FOLK ART. New York: American Studio Books. 1946.

Kenney, John Tarrant. THE HITCHCOCK CHAIR. New York: Clarkson N. Potter, Inc. 1971

Kettell, Russell Hawes. THE PINE FURNITURE OF EARLY NEW ENGLAND. Reprint. New York: Dover Publications, Inc. 1956.

Kirk. John T. EARLY AMERICAN FURNITURE. New York: Alfred A. Knopf. 1970

Meader, Robert F.W. ILLUSTRATED GUIDE TO SHAKER FURNITURE. New York: Dover Publications. 1972

Miller, Edgar G. Jr. AMERICAN ANTIQUE FURNITURE—A BOOK FOR AMATEURS. Two Volumes. Reprint. New York: Dover Publications, Inc. 1966

Montgomery, Charles F. AMERICAN FURNITURE: THE FEDERAL PERIOD. New York: The Viking Press, A Winterthur Book. 1966

Morton, Robert. SOUTHERN ANTIQUES AND FOLK ART. Alabama: Osmoor House, Inc. 1976

Nutting, Wallace. FURNITURE TREASURY. Reprint. New York: The Macmillan Co. 1954

———. FURNITURE OF THE PILGRIM CENTURY. Reprint. New York: Dover Publications, Inc. 1965

———. A WINDSOR HANDBOOK. Reprint. Vermont: Charles E. Tuttle Co. 1973

Philp, Peter and Walkling, Gillian. FIELD GUIDE TO ANTIQUE FURNITURE. New York: Houghton Mifflin Co. 1992

Sack, Albert. FINE POINTS OF FURNITURE: EARLY AMERICAN. New York: Crown Publishers, Inc. 1950

Shea, John G. ANTIQUE COUNTRY FURNITURE OF NORTH AMERICA. New York: Van Nostrand Reinbold Co. 1975

Vandal, Norman. QUEEN ANNE FURNITURE: HISTORY, DESIGN, AND CONSTRUCTION. Connecticut: The Taunton Press. 1990

Watson, Aldren A. COUNTRY FURNITURE. New York: Thomas Y. Crowell Co. 1974

Williams, Derita Coleman and Harsh, Nathan. THE ART AND MYSTERY OF TENNESSEE FURNITURE. Tennessee: Tennessee Historical Society. 1988

Williams, H. Lionel. COUNTRY FURNITURE OF EARLY AMERICA. New Jersey: A.S. Barnes and Co., Inc. 1963